Threads

Threads

PULLING MEANING FROM THE TANGLED MESS

Nancy Kraft

Copyright ©2015 Crone Press. All rights reserved.
ISBN 13: 9780692434642
ISBN: 069243464X
Library of Congress Control Number: 2015907134
Crone Press: Charlotte, North Carolina

For the people of
HOLY TRINITY LUTHERAN CHURCH
Charlotte, North Carolina

Contents

The Way It Is

There's a thread you follow. It goes among
things that change. But it doesn't change.
People wonder about what you are pursuing.
You have to explain the thread.
But it is hard for others to see.
While you hold it you can't get lost.
Tragedies happen; people get hurt
or die; and you suffer and get old.
Nothing you can do can stop time's unfolding.
You don't ever let go of the thread.[1]

The Tangled Mess

❦

I'm not sure when my logical, well-organized world went awry. Despite my best efforts to maintain order, somewhere between childhood and adulthood, it slipped away from me.

Kind of like my necklaces. I used to be very careful with them. I only had a few, so I could hang them neatly in a row. As I accumulated more, it wasn't so easy to keep them all straight. The years went by and this got progressively worse. If you should lift the lid to my jewelry box today, you would see that the necklace situation has gotten completely out of control. You would find a giant glob of gold and silver threads that not even a micro-surgeon could sort through—fine chains woven together so tightly that you can't tell where one begins and the next one ends.

For most of my life, this would have made me crazy. I would have seen it as a problem and gone to work at remedying that problem ASAP. I can remember working relentlessly, for hours, just to unravel one necklace. These days I'm perfectly content leaving that tangled mess sitting just as it is in my jewelry box.

I know this may sound like I've resigned myself to the fact that it's hopeless, but that's not it. The fact is, I find the tangled mess a source of great hope. I can even look at it and smile. The tangled mess of threads has become a metaphor for my life of faith.

Being able to systematically take threads of doctrine and hang them in an orderly row is no longer my task. Picking apart a Biblical text and squeezing every possible drop of truth from it doesn't excite me like it did when I first graduated from seminary. Critically going after people who don't see things my way and proving my point isn't something I feel a need to do any longer. I've grown comfortable with the mess. In fact, I prefer it.

I no longer need to be vigilant about warding off ambiguity, paradox and mystery like unwelcome guests pounding on my door in the middle of the night. For a long time I wouldn't dare open the door, even so much as a crack, lest those midnight marauders invade my dwelling and never leave. Well, that's not the way I live these days. I don't lock the door to my spiritual house anymore. Most of the time, I leave it hanging wide open.

Ambiguity, paradox and mystery are welcome guests. In fact, I'm hoping we can settle down and have a home together. I not only tolerate them in my life, I treasure their company.

That doesn't mean that I ignore the mess. I'm still very much engaged with it. I pick at it and play with it, and every now and then, one of the necklaces begins to break free from the tangles. Admiring the simplicity of the single strand, I study it and slide it between the tips of my fingers. On those rare occasions when I manage to free an entire strand, I might even fasten it around my neck and proudly wear it as a recognition of my accomplishment. I dove into the mess, and I came out with a thread of meaning. Yes!

Some threads of meaning have been gradually emerging from the mess for me. I have yet to see where they end, and I suspect they will continue to free themselves for as long as I live. Threads like: forgiveness, wisdom, compassion and justice. Every time I think I see all the thread has to offer, I learn that there's more to it than I ever had imagined; I wonder what else might remain hidden in the mess, what I might yet discover.

～

When I first began preaching, I believed it was my responsibility to work really hard at studying a Biblical text until I arrived at the absolute truth it revealed. Then I could share that truth with my listeners. I wonder how I ever could have been so presumptuous.

Back in the dark ages when I wrote all my sermons out by hand, I used to save them in a file cabinet with one drawer for each year of the three-year lectionary cycle and a separate file folder for each Sunday. This, I assumed, would save me a lot of needless work over the long haul. When I moved on to the next parish, I could pull out an old sermon, dust it off a bit and preach it again. But that's not how it worked. Instead, each time I pulled out one of my old sermons, I thought, how could I have said that? I would never say that now.

In much the same way that I've found new meaning in Biblical texts through the years, I've found new meaning in my life's story, too. I've revisited the same experiences and interpreted them in entirely new ways at different life stages along the way. The process is never neat and tidy, and it's always evolving. That's what makes the life of faith such a grand adventure.

~

Sometimes we confuse the search for meaning with the desire we have to make sense of life, but they're not the same thing. I've come to the conclusion that life doesn't make a whole lot of sense, at least not from a human perspective. I can't bring myself to believe that everything happens for a reason, or that God manipulates our lives like the parts of an engine so that every little movement has a purpose. Shit happens and I can't begin to understand why.

In the midst of all the randomness of life, even within events that are apparently senseless, there are threads of meaning for those who seek them. Life is more than what appears to be happening on the surface; it can have a deeper meaning for us.

I find meaning in my life from the perspective of a person of faith. I'm sure it's possible to find meaning in other ways, but that will be a story for someone else to tell. Although any faith tradition can provide a framework for finding meaning within the stories of our lives, my faith tradition happens to be Christian. However, I'm not a traditional Christian, particularly in the way the Biblical story informs my life.

Traditionally, Christians have used the Bible as the primary text for interpreting their life experience. They begin with the Biblical story and ask, "How does this apply to my life?" That approach usually leads me to answers for questions I was never asking, so I've flipped the process upside-down.

I start with my own story as the primary text as I seek to understand the deeper meaning of my life. Then I consult the witness of others to see how the meaning they've found might help me in my own search. Among those witnesses who speak to me are the writers of the Bible.

I carry a reservoir of Bible stories within me, and I replenish it on a regular basis. When I draw from that reservoir, the way the Biblical witnesses have made sense of their relationship with God often speaks to my own search for meaning. But I don't stop there. I also pay attention to the witness of other people of faith in other times and places, as well as those who share my life today: my children, clergy in my weekly study group, my faith community, authors who stretch me to think in new ways and any number of people whom I encounter with the expectation that their stories might very well be leading me to new understandings of my own story.

My relationship with others who have stories of their own is a subset of the primary relationship in my life, the one I have with God. God tends to speak to me through other people. Yet without a relationship with God, I would never recognize that.

My relationship with God puts me in an expectant state. I've come to expect God to speak to me through the people and events of my life, not only in ways that are comfortable and cozy, but also in ways that make me squirm like a worm on a hot griddle.

~

I try to approach my days with openness to God speaking to me. That doesn't mean that I expect God to tell me to turn right at an intersection like my GPS. It does mean that somewhere in the tangled mess of my life, there's a grand Thread that's holding everything together, even when it's not apparent to me. I want to be open to that.

Opening myself to God is what I call prayer.

I confess that for much of my adult life I've been disturbed by the whole concept of prayer. It felt like I was telling God what to do, putting God in a subservient position to me. Was it really God's job to serve Nancy's desires like a magic genie in a bottle?

I also used to pray to a God up in heaven who did stuff for us here on earth. My growing understanding of God doesn't fit with that image any more. I've come to see God more present in the here and now than far removed somewhere away beyond the blue.

For a long time I felt so conflicted about prayer that I stopped practicing it altogether. Then I was introduced to contemplative prayer. This way of praying is simply opening myself to God. I offer no instructions for God. I don't bring my agenda to the conversation. I have no expectations for the time we spend together. I put all that aside, take my shoes off and sit with God for a while.

When I first began to practice contemplative prayer, I found myself in tears every time. I felt totally exposed; there was nothing to hide behind. It was just me as God sees me. I wasn't exactly sure how God sees me, but the very thought of it scared me.

In time, the tears subsided, along with the fear. They were replaced with love. Now, I bask in that love.

Along the way, I've grown more honest about myself. That's what happens when you feel completely loved for the person you are without the need to cower behind a façade. As a result, I've revisited the story of my life and found even deeper meaning than I thought possible.

~⁀

Finding the deeper meaning in my life's story is the hardest work I do. The temptation is to take the easy way out and let someone else tell me what it means. But their story isn't my story.

Certainly, my story isn't your story, either. I hope you'll see, within the pages of this book, an invitation to dive deeper into your own story and to be intentional about entering into the search for meaning in your life. I pray you too will experience the grand adventure the life of faith can become when once-hidden truths become revealed along the way.

Scattered Valentines

❧

I couldn't escape the pasty corpse with the ghoulish face and the rubbery fingers that I saw sleeping in a box at the funeral home. At the age of six, my father's dead body relentlessly pursued me.

When I looked up into the windows at night, in the darkness I saw his pallid face staring back at me. I sensed the body lurking in the shadows of the basement and the attic, and I kept my distance. All closets were off limits because I was sure that, if I opened a door, the corpse would fall out on top of me. In my own bedroom, I imagined the dead body stretched out on the top bunk.

My home should have been the safest place I knew. Instead, it became a house of horror.

My family didn't talk about God, nor had I ever been inside a church building. With no faith background, I was deeply troubled about death and thought about it a lot more than any child should. I didn't know what to do with this fear that filled my life.

From the culture around me, I was aware of the concept of God and heaven, and I wanted desperately to believe in both of those things. But when I heard that if I was good, someday I'd get to go to heaven and see my father again, it reminded me too much of Santa Claus. I'd already figured out that Santa was a make-believe person grown-ups invented to keep children in line. Was God just another adult scam like Santa Claus?

This was the first faith crisis I can recall in my life, although I didn't realize it at the time. Within this crisis, I had an awareness of the connection between faith and fear. I remember thinking that if I could really believe in God and heaven, then I wouldn't have to be afraid anymore.

What I didn't quite understand was the nature of faith. I thought it meant knowing something for sure, so I could prove it beyond a doubt. To that end, I decided to run a little experiment in order to find out once and for all if God was real or not.

It was a solid plan. I had an upstairs bedroom that was left undisturbed throughout the day while I was at school; this would be the perfect place for God to leave me a sign. Valentine's Day had just passed, so I had a stack of valentine cards from my classmates that I laid on top of my bedspread, face down, in neat rows. Then I gave my instructions to God: "OK, God. If you're really there, I want you to show me."

I don't know exactly what I expected. Maybe God would spell out *Hi!* with the cards, or he would turn some of them over. I didn't have a specific sign in mind, but I was hoping for something that would tell me God was more than a variation on Santa Claus. I needed a sign that God was real.

That afternoon, as I was walking home from school, I was anxious to see what was waiting for me on my bed. I was also a little afraid because I was finally going to know for sure if there really was a God, and I sensed that what I found on my bed could change my whole life.

As I opened the front door to the house, my black cocker spaniel Inky greeted me. He was so glad to see me that he jumped up to lick my face. Any other day, that's when I would get down on the floor with him and scratch his belly in tiny circles until I found the magic switch that connected the electric current to his leg and made it twitch uncontrollably. But I didn't have time for Inky today; I needed to get to my bedroom.

When Inky saw me walking in that direction he bounded up the stairs ahead of me, jumped up on my bed before I had the chance to get there, and the valentines flew all over the room.

"Inky, look what you've done!"

When I realized that I would never know if God had given me a sign with the cards I left on my bed, I wept. This had been my one chance, and I wouldn't try again. If God had answered my prayer, I couldn't very well go back to him and ask him to do it all over again, and if God hadn't answered my prayer, I would never have a way of knowing.

~

I wasn't the first person who ever questioned God's presence in the world. It seems to be common enough that I'd call it a universal experience. Stories of similar struggles are told throughout the pages of the Bible.

One of my favorites is the story of the whiny Israelites in the desert with Moses in Exodus 17:1-7.

The Israelites were chronic complainers, and for good reason. They'd been slaves in Egypt, but at least as slaves they knew what to expect, and there was some security in that. Then, along comes this guy Moses, and he's bound and determined to free them.

In the beginning, Moses thinks he can just stroll on up to Pharaoh, say, "Let my people go," and Pharaoh will reply, "Sure." But he soon learns that Pharaoh is a hard sell. Not even a series of horrible plagues can convince him: water turned to blood, frogs, gnats, flies, diseased livestock, boils, thunder and hail, locusts and darkness. It's all pretty nasty stuff.

Then there is one more plague, and it promises to be the nastiest of all. The firstborn in every household is going to be killed. No family will be able to escape it—except the families of the slaves. Moses offers them a way out.

All they have to do is go along with the plan Moses lays out for them. Given the alternative, why wouldn't they? So, they're in. They do exactly what Moses instructs them to do. Each household kills a lamb and uses the blood to mark their door so the angel of death will pass over them.

Now, if you take this to mean that they're good, God-fearing people, I wouldn't be so quick to conclude that. It's more likely that they're just plain old fearing people who don't want their children to die.

Next comes the dramatic exit from Egypt where the slaves escape through the Red Sea. They have no idea how Moses pulls that one off. It's way cool! But then when they end up in the wilderness with no food, the coolness factor quickly disappears.

The Israelites grumble, "We must have been crazy to follow this guy. Here we had all that we wanted to eat in Egypt. Now he leads us out into the middle of nowhere so we can starve to death!" They whine and complain until Moses can't stand it anymore.

Once again, God comes to the rescue; he sends them manna and quail and saves the day, just in time for the next crisis.

The Israelites find themselves in the middle of the desert, and they're about to die of thirst. How could they have left their homes in Egypt, which means *land of many waters*, only to end up in this godforsaken place with nothing to drink? Once again, they whine and complain to Moses. Actually, it's a little stronger than that this time. The text from Exodus tells us they *quarreled* with Moses.

Moses says to them, "Why do you quarrel with me? Why do you test the Lord?"

The people come back at Moses. "Why did you bring us out of Egypt, to kill us and our children and livestock with thirst?"

So, Moses cries out to the Lord, "What shall I do with these people? They are almost ready to stone me!"

Notice that he asks God to help him. He doesn't tell God what to do. He doesn't demand water. He asks for help. He doesn't give God direction; he asks God for guidance. What shall I do with these people?

God tells Moses to take some of the elders with him, along with the staff he used to strike the Nile, and go to a place where they will see God standing before them on a rock.

When they find God standing on the rock, Moses strikes it with his staff and water comes gushing out. The story concludes with Moses naming the place Massah and Meribah because the Israelites quarreled and tested the Lord, saying, "Is the Lord among us or not?"

Under the circumstances, it's a legitimate question: Is the Lord among us or not? It's hard to see that God is with you when you're about to die of thirst. You remember better times and you see how it is now, and you think, you're following God, so how can this be happening? Is the Lord among us or not?

A big question I have of this story is: Why do the people have to come to Moses and tell him they're thirsty? I mean, doesn't Moses notice the lack of water? Isn't he thirsty himself? Again and again in the Exodus story, the Israelites fret over stuff that Moses hardly notices. They may be in the same location, but they clearly are living in two different realities.

The Israelites have no relationship with God. When they're in trouble, they don't complain to God; they complain to Moses. They're 40 years away from having a relationship with God. They can only believe God is present when they're getting what they want. When things aren't going their way, they have to ask, "Is the Lord among us or not?"

Moses has a different way of seeing the circumstances of his life. Whether God is doing what he wants or not, Moses always knows God is present. Because, unlike the Israelites, Moses and God have a relationship with one another.

When God sends Moses out to find water, he tells Moses that he will stand before him. Jewish sages teach that the Hebrew word for standing in this text, *amidah*, refers to prayer. As Moses comes prepared to stand before God in prayer, God stands before Moses. Moses brings his whole being to the encounter, and God is present in this holy moment, too. They stand before one another reverently, present to one another.

Is the Lord among us or not? For the Israelites, it's a fair question to ask, and the question remains. For Moses, as one who is in relationship with God, the question is answered even before it's asked: Absolutely, the Lord is present.

We all have moments when we ask, "Is the Lord among us or not?" We may need proof. We may expect God to jump through our hoops and deliver. If he doesn't, we conclude that either he doesn't exist or he doesn't care. But when we're in a relationship with God, when we've experienced God standing before us, God present with us, we don't ask God to prove himself in those moments that test us. Instead, we do what Moses did; we ask God to help us.

~

Those many years ago when I summoned God's presence through an experiment with valentines in my bedroom may seem like a silly little childish activity that I should have forgotten by now, but it continues to be one of the most significant events of my life. From my perspective back then, as a first-grader, unless God could prove to me that he was real, he wasn't. I know that sounds pretty hard-nosed for a child, but that's the way I thought.

I don't think that way anymore. Now when I look back on that childhood experiment in my bedroom, I'm certain that God was present.

What's changed? Well, obviously, I've experienced an entire lifetime between then and now. I've spent the better part of that lifetime studying, reflecting and speculating about God. It's been my life's work. But none of that really changed the way I came to see the presence of God in those scattered valentines. It took growing into a living relationship with God for me to find new meaning in that childhood experience.

I'm not sure when that relationship actually began. I know the official answer is that it all began at baptism, but since I was baptized when I was 16, I could never say that I was on my own all those years up until then. I was a child of God, even though I had no awareness of it. And to be honest, I didn't notice a big change in my awareness after I was baptized. I continued to wonder if God was real or not. More than anything, I wanted to believe it. I fervently prayed to believe it, often soaking my pillow with tears at night, but I just couldn't bring myself to go there. The whole idea was too preposterous to me.

I waited for God to show me a sign, to convince me that he was real. Nothing short of divine intervention was going to do it for me. Then I got tired of waiting for something that was never going to happen. It seemed pointless, like hanging out at the airport waiting for a paper airplane to arrive from Mars.

I concluded that God was a fictitious character lesser people needed as a crutch because they were too weak to make it on their own. I had wasted enough time fretting over such foolishness. So, I moved on and scarcely gave the whole God thing another thought. I busied myself with more important adolescent activities like hanging out with my friends, chugging beer and making out with boys.

That's when God came after me. What began as a gentle nudge, eventually escalated to a smack upside the head.

As a college freshman, I'd been randomly thrown into a dorm room with three women who were strangers to me. It turned out they all happened to be Christians who went to church on Sundays. Despite their invitations, I declined to join them.

While I was studying at the Student Union, a group of students plopped down at the table next to me and opened their Bibles. I pretended to study as I listened to every word they were saying.

I went on a picnic at a park with friends and noticed a group of seemingly normal people gathering under the shelter beside us. Then they started singing hymns.

When I returned to my dorm after working the breakfast shift in the cafeteria, someone was being baptized in the pond outside my door.

I met a young man and was drawn to his gentle spirit and pure heart. I didn't find out that he was a Pentecostal Christian until after I fell madly in love with him.

Enough already!

Now, here's the thing. I went to Bowling Green *State* University. This wasn't a church school, and yet Christians were constantly in my face. It was too much. Then I started to feel like God was in my face, too. Everywhere I turned, God was saying, "Here I am, Nancy."

When I looked at window panes, I saw crosses. Were they really there, or was I a woman obsessed? I couldn't tell if I was having a mystical experience and God was speaking to me, or I was losing my mind.

I was hungry for answers to questions I'd never had much interest in asking before, and I wondered if God was calling me to go to seminary after college.

Night after night, I went to study at the library and ended up wandering into the stacks of religion books, pulling one or two off the shelves, getting lost in their pages, until a woman announced, "The library will close in ten minutes."

Sometimes in my dreams, I heard a voice calling my name so audibly that I answered. How was it possible that God had been silent all this time, and now he wouldn't give me a moment's peace? The more I tried to ignore him, the more aggressively he seemed to come after me. I feared that if I didn't acknowledge his presence, I was going to go mad. So I did. Acknowledge his presence, that is.

Of course, acknowledging someone exists hardly constitutes having a relationship with him or her. But it's a start.

Like Other Women Change Shoes

❧❧

Eighteen years ago I died in Ohio and was resurrected in North Carolina.

In my former life, I had a husband, Will. He and I met in seminary, and we were married for 20 years. Together we had two children and co-pastored a thriving congregation. I suspect that many people who knew me envied my life. I actually thought it was a pretty good life myself until I learned that, beneath the surface, something very sick was going on.

They always say the wife knows when her husband is unfaithful, even if she won't admit it to herself, but honestly, I didn't know.

Will had some close relationships with women friends through the years, but it never occurred to me that he was capable of adultery. How could he possibly do such a thing, then stand in the pulpit on Sunday mornings and preach? It was incomprehensible to me. So when Will told me that he was going to leave me to begin a new life with a parishioner, a woman who was also married with two children, I was in complete shock. This couldn't be happening. But it was.

Did he really understand what he was saying? Did he know what his life would be like if he followed through with his plan? How did he think our children would respond to this? Was he naïve enough to believe he would be able to pastor another church with his new wife by his side? I grilled him with questions.

Instead of answering my questions, Will cried—a lot. He was so fragile that I feared he might have a breakdown and end up in the psych ward. And yet, he didn't waver in his desire to be with the other woman.

I suspected Will was depressed, and having lived through clinical depression myself, I was well aware of how it can serve up a dish of scrambled brains in your head. I was convinced that he would wake up some morning, after he had thrown his life away, and say, "Oh, my God, what have I done?"

So, I offered him a proposal: "If you'll see a counselor and get on anti-depressants, in six weeks, if you still want to leave, I won't fight you." He agreed to do that.

At the end of six weeks, Will was in a completely different place. The two of us started seeing his counselor together, and we were closer than we'd ever been. We even took a romantic trip to the Virgin Islands where we spent our days snorkeling in the ocean together and our nights rekindling our passion for one another. It felt like we were going to make it.

Then the sky fell in.

The woman my husband had been involved with reported him to the bishop, who called Will into his office and confronted him on the allegations against him. Will confessed that they were true, and the bishop asked him to resign, both from the congregation he and I were serving together and from our denomination's clergy roster.

The bishop asked Will to resign immediately by sending a letter to the congregation. Will complied. But when the bishop read Will's letter, he wasn't satisfied with the ambiguous wording, so he informed Will that he wanted him to tell the congregation exactly why he was resigning on the next Sunday morning at worship. He also wanted to hear what Will said, and if he wasn't satisfied with how Will explained his actions, he would come the following Sunday to do it for him.

Some difficult conversations followed—between Will and me, with our teenage children, with friends, with congregational leaders.

I remember walking through it all much the way I had seen so many women react to the death of a spouse. The reality of the situation doesn't really sink in. Instead, they busy themselves with attending to necessary details and taking care of everyone around them. That worked for me. I had plenty to keep me distracted from the hurt and grief I carried inside. Not only did I have my children to look after, but my congregation as well.

Somehow we all made it through the Sunday morning when Will publicly confessed his transgressions. He did it in the sermon. I led the liturgy and excused myself when it came time for him to preach. I heard it all, but from a seat in the narthex, behind the congregation, not front-and-center where people could scrutinize the wounded wife's reaction to every word her adulterous husband uttered.

The night before this was to happen, we gave our children, who were then in high school, a preview of coming attractions, and we offered them the option of staying home. They chose to be present to support their father, so they were in the audience for one of our performances. I suspect that to their dying day they will remember it, as will everyone who was in attendance that day.

We acted out this tragedy not once, but three times, at each of our Sunday morning worship services. Our audience responded with tears for Will and anger directed toward the woman who had reported him to the bishop. One of the older members announced after worship, in a voice loud enough for all to hear, "All I want to know is, who *was* the bitch?" (Typically, the victim is perceived as the villain in these scenarios.)

Through it all, I publicly vowed that I would stand by my man. I assured the congregation that I had already forgiven Will, and we were going to get past this.

The next Sunday, Will stayed home while I led worship solo. Standing before a congregation that hung on my every word, I was amazing. Everybody told me so.

I felt invincible. I could handle this. I could be the woman who overcame overwhelming adversity and inspired everyone around her. I could care for my husband and my children and my congregation and the whole damn world if necessary. I was the Woman of Steel!

Over the next few months, I learned that my husband had fooled around with more than one woman. To say that I was struggling to trust him again is an understatement. Then he did the absolute worst thing he possibly could have done at the time—he lied to me.

A member of the congregation had a heart attack and died while I was away on a retreat. When I learned of it, after I got back into town on Saturday afternoon, I ran over to see the widow, and I spent some time with her.

By the time I returned home, I could hardly talk because I'd come down with a terrible cold, and I was losing my voice. I drugged myself with Nyquil and crawled into bed, hoping that between the drug and a good night's sleep, I'd be able to speak for worship services the next day.

On Sunday morning, I opened my mouth and was relieved to hear audible words coming out. I also learned that while I was sleeping soundly the night before, Wanda, the widow of the man who died, had been taken to the emergency room for chest pains. Will told me I had received a call about it, and he didn't want to wake me. By the time I learned of it, she was already home and doing well.

A couple of weeks after I did her husband's funeral, I followed up with a visit to Wanda. As I was standing in the doorway exchanging parting words with her, she said, "Oh, and please tell Will how much I appreciated him coming to the emergency room. It meant so much to me."

"*My* Will was with you at the hospital?"

"Yes. Please thank him for me."

I knew nothing of this. Will told me Wanda was at the hospital, but not that he went to see her there, and I understood why.

He knew how wrong it was for him to provide pastoral care within the congregation he no longer pastored, particularly under the circumstances that led to his resignation. There had been other occasions when he wanted to jump in and act as pastor to a church member, and I had to insist that he maintain the necessary boundaries. It was a painful issue between us. I resented him for putting me in the position of being the enforcer of pastoral ethics that he clearly understood, but chose to ignore.

Now this. Did he really think I wasn't going to find out? Did he not realize that the worst thing he could do to our precarious relationship was lie to me?

Trust had been shot to pieces, and the damage was irreparable. Despite the fact that I had vowed I would stand by my man, he gave me no other choice but to ask him to move out. It was over.

And the story goes downhill from there.

I was determined to maintain my superhero status, despite this setback. I never took a Sunday off. I saw a counselor, although I didn't feel it was necessary. I was doing just fine. I pressed on, never really dealing with what had happened to my life. I was like someone suffering from post-traumatic stress disorder who continues to stuff reality deep inside because it's too painful to face. Over the next few months, the reality of my damaged life simmered its way to a slow boil until, without warning, it blew.

~

Shortly before my divorce became final, a former high school boyfriend came back into my life and swept me off my feet. Stan Turner had a crush on me all through high school. We went to prom together. The night before I married Will, Stan called me on the phone and tried to talk me out of it. Now after all these years, he was back in my life, confessing his undying love for me.

I couldn't resist. I was like a dried up desert, and Stan came washing over me like a tidal wave. It was all terribly romantic, and then I did something terribly terrible. And stupid. More red flags were waving than you'd see in a Chinese military parade, but I ignored them all, and I married him.

There was a huge problem with this so-called marriage. I came to learn that Stan was already married to someone else, and he had a family in California. Yes, I married a bigamist.

My so-called marriage lasted about a year-and-a-half with a man who never really lived with me. And all this, with my congregation and the entire synod tuned into my life like they were watching reality TV.

~

I needed to start over someplace where no one knew me. Since I'd always loved North Carolina and thought I might like to retire there someday, I decided to make the transition a little earlier than anticipated, and I moved to Charlotte. I also returned to my maiden name of *Kraft* and started coloring my hair red. I imagined it was a little like joining the witness protection program. This was a whole new me with a whole new life. So I thought.

One of the first things I did after I moved to North Carolina was attend a spirituality retreat that the synod was sponsoring. The organizers sent out a list of participants in advance, and I noticed that a woman from my past, Jane, would be attending. She had chaired the search committee at a congregation where I interviewed in North Carolina before I decided to come to Advent, Charlotte.

Jane was the first person I saw when I arrived for the retreat. "Why, Nancy Turner, I didn't know you were going to be here!"

Turner had been my name when I interviewed at her church, the name I took from my bigamist husband, so I explained to her, "That's because that's not my name anymore. I was divorced, and I've gone back to using my maiden name, *Kraft*."

Jane was still standing there chatting with me when a pastor I knew from Ohio, someone who had moved south several years before I did, walked in the door. He took one look at me and said, "Nancy Sturgis! I didn't know you were going to be here!" *Sturgis* had been my last name when I was married to husband numero uno.

"That's because my name isn't *Sturgis* anymore, it's *Kraft*," I told him.

At that, Jane turned to me and said, "Wow, Nancy! You change names like other women change shoes!"

Never in my life had I ever imagined such a moment.

A change of geography wasn't going to change my past. I had messed up—big time. I had no idea I was capable of so royally messing up, but the evidence was irrefutable. I changed names like other women changed shoes. Lord, have mercy.

꩜

I developed a special affinity for the apostle Peter when my life fell apart. Of all the screw ups in the Bible, and there are plenty of them, he's at the top of the list.

He had been one of Jesus' closest friends, and yet, when it was all about to come down, Jesus predicted that Peter was going to deny him three times. Peter insisted that he would never do such a thing. He would never betray Jesus like that. He couldn't!

But it happened just as Jesus said it would. When they came to arrest Jesus, Peter darted off like a startled rabbit. Then when Peter was asked if he was one of Jesus' followers, he denied even so much as knowing the man—three times.

How could he ever get past his betrayal? Would he ever be able to recover from this, or would he forever be known as Jesus' friend who stabbed in the back three times?

After the resurrection, Peter and his friends returned to the occupation they had known before their rabbi Jesus called them to be his students, fishing. One morning as they were pulling their nets up out of the sea, they saw a man on the shore preparing breakfast over a charcoal fire. It turned out to be Jesus and the meal was for them.

While they were eating, Jesus asked Peter, "Do you love me?"

Peter responded with tears in his eyes. "Yes, Lord, you know that I love you."

Now, considering their history, Jesus could easily have come back with, "You love me? Well, you sure coulda fooled me!" Instead, he chose to free Peter from the shame of his past.

Three times Jesus asked Peter, "Do you love me?" The question wasn't spoken in judgment, but as absolution, three times, in order to wipe away Peter's three denials so he could be restored: to himself, to Jesus, to his community.

But Peter wasn't simply forgiven and restored. Jesus had more than that in mind for him. He told Peter to feed his sheep, commissioning Peter to carry on as the shepherd in his absence. This was not to make amends for his past. Jesus forgave him, unconditionally. But he wanted Peter to see that his life in the future wouldn't be defined by his past. No one could change the past. Not even Jesus' forgiveness could change what Peter had done. What changed though, by Jesus' forgiveness, was Peter's future.

This was the text (John 21:15-17) that I chose to have read at my ordination service. My husband Will was the preacher. That day, I never could have imagined all that this story would come to mean to me. When I was 26 years old, I only read it as Jesus telling Peter to take over for him, to become a shepherd for Jesus' sheep. I thought that's what it meant for me to be a pastor, too—to shepherd Jesus' sheep.

I didn't consider the depth of the relationship between Peter and Jesus, the history they had with one another. Now when I read this text from John's gospel, that's all I can see. It's a story of forgiveness. It's about the gift of a future to someone who carries a heavy past.

～

Through the years, I've met a lot of folks who believe that all they ever will be has already been determined because of some screw-up from their past. The memory of their past failure seems to have a grip on their lives. They resign themselves to the identity their past has imposed on them. Because of their past, they live as if their future has already been decided.

But here's the thing. While it's true that we all carry our past failures around with us, we get to decide how we will frame our past. Will we use it to block ourselves from living into the future, or can our past failures be redeemed and used as a source of healing and wholeness?

Like Peter, God has forgiven my failures and redeemed my past, renewing me in my calling. Even though I can't change my past, by God's grace, it doesn't determine my future. Instead, because of all I've learned from my failures, and my disappointments, and my dumb-ass decisions, the past has transformed my future.

When I look at the meaning of my life from the perspective of one who is included in God's loving embrace, no matter what my past may be, I can't lose.

A Goose Tail in the Woods

❦

$\mathcal{B}$ ack when I was living in Uniontown, Ohio, about 20 years ago, an amusing phenomenon was going on. Everywhere you looked, someone had a concrete goose sitting on their front porch. They were painted white, with an orange beak, and they stood just about the same height as a real goose. Now, the fun part was that people couldn't allow them to stand there naked, so they dressed them. In fact, there was a whole cottage industry for selling concrete goose costumes.

I used to think they were the silliest things and often remarked about them to my parishioners. "Did you see the goose on the corner dressed like a pink flamingo?" "How 'bout that goose dressed like Abraham Lincoln?"

Apparently, I commented about them one too many times. The people in my church concluded that I must like them, so they surprised me and gave me one. It was wearing a blue and white gingham dress and a yellow straw hat.

Because the new goose was given in love, I felt compelled to put it out in front my house. Of course, I had to dress it: like a pumpkin, a turkey, Santa, a leprechaun, an Easter bunny. When my daughter graduated from high school, I bought a cap and gown for it to wear. In the summer it had a little Cleveland Indians uniform.

When I received a call to serve at a church in North Carolina, I had no intention of bringing the goose with me. But there was a problem. People from my new church and some from my old church got together and loaded the moving van for me. They were just about to close the door to the van when one of them shouted, "Oh, don't forget the goose!" And on the van it went.

I moved the goose to my new home in North Carolina, where people knew nothing of concrete geese. It embarrassed me, and I never once dressed it. It sat there naked on my porch for a year-and-a-half until it was time for me to move to my new condo, and believe me, I wasn't about to move that goose with me again. It was time to dump the goose.

Now I had a new problem. Do you have any idea how difficult it is to dispose of a concrete goose? I couldn't lift it, and I certainly couldn't throw it in the trash can. I had to devise another method of disposal—one I could manage myself.

Next to my house there was a little wooded lot. I dragged the goose into the trees and dug a deep hole. I scooted the goose right up to the edge, tipped it over, and it dove head first into the earth. Then I filled in the hole with dirt. That's when I noticed that I hadn't dug deep enough, and there it was—a little bit of the tail, maybe an inch or two, poking up through the earth.

Well, that's how it was going to stay. There was no way I could extract a twenty-ton goose from the ground without a backhoe. I was done with the damn thing!

I often think about that little white goose tail sticking up in the woods. I imagine someone tripping over it someday and wondering, "What the hell is that?" Then maybe they'll dig it up. It might be some archeologist a thousand years from now, and she'll speculate about how one of those strange concrete images they found in the area formerly known as Ohio ended up 500 miles to the south. For the fact is, even though I was done with the damn goose, it's still there. And now someone in the future will have to deal with it.

As strange as it may sound, the concrete goose I had so much trouble dumping from my life held meaning for me. I moved to North Carolina to begin my life again, but I came with heavy baggage from my former life in Ohio. The metaphor was clear.

In time, the original meaning I derived from the episode of the concrete goose evolved. My interpretation isn't all about me and my stuff anymore.

I think about all those who will come after us and what we'll be leaving behind for them. Will they be stumbling over the stuff we tried to cover up, but couldn't? Will they be living on a sustainable planet? Will they be cleaning up our mess? Will they be further buried in the consumerism that consumes us?

Another meaning I've drawn from the goose tail has nothing to do with physical stuff. I consider other things my generation has brought with us from the past that we'll leave behind for future generations to deal with. Will they try to solve the world's problems through violence because that's the only way we've taught them? Will they be fueled by hatred and fear? Or will they learn from us a better way, a way of compassion and understanding?

All that from a goose tail in the woods. It's such a rush when I'm able to derive meaning from something senseless. This makes up for all the times I dig deep to find meaning in my life and come up empty.

~

It was so unlike Cathy to show up late for choir practice. She was, after all, the choir director.

I tried calling her and got no answer. Where was she?

A choir member, Lou, and I decided to run up to her house to see if she was all right. She had been sick a couple of days before, and I hadn't spoken to her. Perhaps she had taken some medicine that made her oversleep.

When Lou and I arrived at Cathy's house, her car was in the garage. We looked in through the front door and could see the TV on and half of an uneaten dinner sitting on the coffee table. We rang the doorbell, pounded on the door and called out her name. Nothing.

We walked around the house, straining to look through the windows, hoping to find her. When we got to her bedroom, Lou cried out, "She's on the floor!" We could see her feet extended from the other side of the bed.

Lou broke the glass, we climbed in through the window, and there she was, stretched out on the floor, face down. When I touched her, she was as cold as concrete in January.

Cathy had been much more than the church's director of music to me. We were close in age, both of us were single, and we spent a lot of time together. When she took me fishing with her, she cheerfully threaded the worm on the hook for me without judging me for my wimpy-ness. If that's not a true friend, I don't know what is.

I preached for Cathy's funeral at the church, and then I went to her home in West Virginia and preached there as well. For the life of me I can't remember how I found anything meaningful to say.

It made no sense to me; it wasn't supposed to happen. Cathy was only in her early 40s, and without warning, she had a fatal stroke. Even though more than a decade has passed, I've never been able to extract a single thread of meaning from it.

What the heck was that supposed to mean? I like to believe that every apparently meaningless thing has some potential for meaning.

I've never been able to find a speck of meaning in Cathy's death. And yet I know that, even when I'm unable to discover any meaning, that doesn't necessarily mean it isn't there. I've filed the experience away and return to it from time to time, hoping that, in retrospect, something hidden may yet become visible for me.

~

When I was younger, I always thought that the whole point of the spiritual journey was to learn and grow so that I would come to understand the stuff that befuddled me. If I read my Bible and studied and prayed and listened to what God was saying to me, then gradually, I'd start to get a clue, and eventually, I'd find clarity. If I worked hard enough at it, as I got older, I would finally come to understand those spiritual secrets that seemed to elude me when I was younger, and that's when I would become the wise old woman I aspired to be.

I thought of the Holy Spirit as God's teacher in my life, but more than a typical teacher, the Holy Spirit had the power to make me learn, whether I was receptive to the teaching or not. When I was too thick-headed to comprehend the truth God was trying to impart, the Holy Spirit would do what needed to be done so I could receive it. Like Jesus' parable where the seed is planted in the fertile soil, the Holy Spirit would cultivate my brain, softening it up to receive the seed. In time, the Holy

Spirit, my own personal tutor, would lead me to true wisdom. That's how I thought it would work for me.

In reality, I do feel that I've grown wiser as I've grown in years, but wisdom doesn't look anything like I thought it would. It has little to do with gaining knowledge, or being able to finally answer those questions that keep me awake nights. It's more like the tangled mess of silver and gold threads in my jewelry box.

As much as I've worked at untangling the mess, it seems that the best I can do is pick at it. Through the years, I've come to see the mess, not as a problem to be conquered, but as a gift to be cherished. I wasn't created to clean it up, explain it, or control it, just as I wasn't created to become pure and holy, to strive for godly perfection or to bring order out of chaos. I wasn't created *apart* from the mess; I was created *a part of* the mess. But I am not a mess, because God is not a mess, and I am created in the image of God.

I've struggled to understand what it might mean to be created in the image of God, and it seems to me that whatever it is, it sets us humans apart from the rest of creation.

For a long time I thought the difference was that humans are capable of love and animals aren't. Then I started living with a dog and that theory was shot to pieces; I have no doubt that she can love.

Now I'm thinking that what sets us humans apart is our capacity for meaning-making. I don't think animals spend a whole lot of time reflecting on the deeper meaning of their lives. Of course, when I watch reality TV, I'm not always convinced that some people do either. But it seems that most of the people I spend my days with are in the midst of a struggle to find meaning in their lives, and they're hoping that the meaning they find will draw them closer to God. I'm not talking about people who get excited about seeing the figure of Jesus in a tortilla or Mary in a grilled cheese sandwich. I'm talking about people who are looking for God in the deeper places of their lives.

That's not to say that we can ever see things as God does, or that we can ever really know the absolute, definitive meaning of our lives. But we want to, and we struggle to, and that makes us unique in all creation. We think about such things. We even think about thinking. And think about thinking about thinking. And ... well, you get my point.

~

As I struggle to find meaning in my life, I see my days on this planet unfolding as a story with a beginning, a middle and an end. That story only makes sense to me within the context of an even larger story.

My faith provides me with a larger story. It's a story I share with other people of faith, as well. That's why being part of a faith community is essential for me. I need to be with other people who share a common story for their lives.

My larger faith story is the Jesus story. It's certainly not the only faith story in the world, but it's the one that carries the deepest truth for me. It's the story of finding my true self by losing my false self. It's the story of trusting in the freeing love of God above all that would enslave me: fear, shame, pride, self-protectiveness. It's the story of finding healing and wholeness in the midst of my brokenness. It's the story of death and resurrection.

That's my larger story. It's what makes sense for me. Without it, I don't know if I could continue slogging along through this world. What would be the point of it all?

A lot of people today find life meaningless because their lives have no context. They only have their individual stories to examine; there's no larger story to make sense of their lives. They've attached themselves to a story that's so small it can't possibly contain all the depth of their experience.

Socrates once wrote, "The unexamined life is not worth living." I suspect that he was right insofar as if we examine our lives and find no meaning in them, they're literally meaningless. That's why I believe what I do as a pastor is so important. I'm someone who helps people examine their lives. Because of the larger story that I'm a part of, I can offer a framework for them to find meaning in their lives.

All people of faith can help folks examine their lives, no matter what their larger story might be. That's why I feel a special bond with rabbis, priests, monks, shamans, imams and other such people God has chosen to guide others in their search for meaning.

We're all in this together. No matter what the larger story is that we find to make sense of our lives, there's an even larger story than that, a meta-story that contains all our larger stories. We may not be able to grasp it with our limited human perspective, but it's the Story that ultimately unites all of us meaning-makers.

Maybe that's what it means to be created in the image of God. We're not, each of us, little images of God, but collectively, we are the Image of God—together.

∼

"We know that all things work together for good for those who love God, who are called according to his purpose" (Romans 8:28). Early in my faith journey, I liked to believe that everything happens for a reason, that it's all a part of God's grand design. That brought me comfort and security, especially when my fears seemed overwhelming.

I don't believe that anymore. I can't say that everything happens for a reason. There are too many things that happen in this world that have no redeeming value: the slaughter of innocent children at an elementary school, an earthquake that kills thousands of people, a genocidal holocaust that eliminates millions of lives. I cannot conclude that somehow God made any of these things happen for a purpose. That makes no sense to me.

However, within such events, there's the opportunity for struggle, self-examination, and perhaps a revealed truth or two along the way. Even within the most senseless events in our lives, there is the potential to find meaning.

I don't know that I would put it quite the way Paul did. All things work together for good? Not exactly. How about: As long as there is the potential for meaning, some of the most senseless things can work together for good.

I resonate with the words of one of the characters in Susan Howatch's novel, *Absolute Truths*, a sculptor, who observed: "So in the end every major disaster, every tiny error, every wrong turning, every fragment of discarded clay, all the blood, sweat and tears—everything has meaning. I give it meaning. I reuse, reshape, recast all that goes wrong so that in the end nothing is wasted and nothing is without significance and nothing ceases to be precious to me."[2]

Yes, even a goose tail in the woods.

---

2 (New York: Knopf, 1995)

Clorox Only Makes It Worse

❧

*D*uring my brief experience with the church as a teenager, I learned that I am a sinner. This came as news to me. Although, the idea that I do bad things was something I'd been dealing with for years, the word *sinner* was foreign to me. Am I a sinner? Really?

I could never understand why the adults around me made such a big freakin' deal out of some of the things I did. Like the time I picked the neighbor's flowers. Or when my best friend Jeanne and I got caught with our shorts down leaning against the house. Or when I built a dam in front of the sewer at the end of our street. Adults let me know that I was a bad girl for doing these things.

I didn't honestly feel like a bad girl myself. From my perspective, I had a perfectly logical reason for everything. I picked the neighbor's flowers to give them to my mom. I pulled my shorts down on the side of the house because I needed to relieve my bladder. And, when I built that dam in the gutter, it was because I wanted to make a little pond to play in, and every time I tried to do it with sticks and mud, it got washed away. So I *had* to build it with the concrete mix I found in the basement. I honestly thought my parents would praise me for being so smart and resourceful. But, oh, my! You would have thought I was ready for juvie it was such a big deal. I didn't get it.

When I sat in a church pew for the first time at the age of 13, once again, adults were telling me that I do bad things. I figured that if they were saying it in church there must be some truth to it, so I received this information with my head, but I couldn't bring myself to accept it with my heart. Other people did bad things; that was clear to me. But it took me years to see how this sinner thing had any connection with me.

~

I was not yet 30 years old, a young mother and a young pastor in my first call. My daughter Gretchen was four, and my son Ben was eighteen months old. I had the life I'd always dreamt of, and I felt there was no limit to what I could accomplish, although keeping up with a large parish and two very active little ones, I was often harried.

One night when my husband and I were preparing to go out to an international potluck with some other pastors in the area, we were running late, as usual. We needed to give the kids a bath before we left, and we needed to prepare something to bring to the potluck, so my husband took bathroom duty and I started cooking.

I poured oil into the wok to heat it up while I began wrapping egg rolls. Since the counter was covered with dirty dishes, and I didn't have time to deal with them, I scooted them aside and made myself a small work space alongside the electric wok. I was so frazzled that I wasn't paying close attention, and I did something that I knew I should never do—I left the cord to the wok hanging over the kitchen counter.

Out of the corner of my eye, I saw Ben trotting into the kitchen buck naked; he had escaped from his father. I stood about a yard away as I watched his chubby little hand tug on the electric cord to the wok. It happened so fast, but I remember watching it like it was in slow motion. There was nothing I could do. Hot oil landed on Ben's head and ran down his back.

This was just the beginning of a long, painful journey. One thing led to another and we spent years in hospitals dealing with the devastating results of Ben's burn. To this day, I seldom see him without a hat. The accident affected his life in profound ways and mine, too.

While we were going through all of this, there was no disputing one critical fact: It had been my fault. Sure it was an accident, but it was an accident that was caused by my stupidity and my carelessness.

This was the first time I had ever seen myself as a Psalm 51 kind of sinner.

~

David seemed to live one of those charmed lives. In the eyes of everyone around him he was successful and had all that a man could want, but he wasn't satisfied. He discovered something he couldn't have, and that made him want it all the more.

That something was a woman. She was married to another man, but David wanted her, so he took her. He seduced her and raped her. Then she became pregnant.

Now David had to have both the woman and the baby, and he would do anything to make that happen, even commit murder. So he tricked the woman's husband into going to the place where his killer was waiting for him. Then David married the man's wife, the woman who was carrying David's child. Nice guy, huh?

The David in this story is none other than King David in the Bible. After he did this despicable thing, God sent his prophet Nathan to tell him just how wretched he was. Nathan pronounced judgment on David, and tradition has it that it was on this occasion that David wrote Psalm 51:

> *Have mercy on me, O God, according to your steadfast love;*
> *according to your abundant mercy blot out my*
> *transgressions.*
> *Wash me thoroughly from my iniquity, and cleanse me*
> *from my sin.*

For I know my transgressions, and my sin is ever before me.

Against you, you alone, have I sinned, and done what is evil in your sight,

so that you are justified in your sentence and blameless when you pass judgment.

Indeed, I was born guilty, a sinner when my mother conceived me.

You desire truth in the inward being; therefore teach me wisdom in my secret heart.

Purge me with hyssop, and I shall be clean; wash me, and I shall be whiter than snow.

Let me hear joy and gladness; let the bones that you have crushed rejoice.

Hide your face from my sins, and blot out all my iniquities.

Create in me a clean heart, O God, and put a new and right spirit within me.

We liturgical types begin the season of Lent every year reading Psalm 51 on Ash Wednesday. After all of our wandering and straying from God's path throughout the year, Lent comes to us prodigals once again, calling us home.

What was true for David is true for us as well. We may work hard to convince the world, and maybe even ourselves, that we have it all together, but inside even the most beautiful people, there is some ugliness.

The burn to Ben's head led me to see how I stand in solidarity with everyone else who makes up our broken humanity. I am capable of doing something horrific. I have no doubt about that now. I cannot look at those I so easily had labeled sinners through the eyes of pity or contempt as I once did. That's no longer possible, not now that I see myself standing beside them.

It took messing up big, like David, for me to see this.

I know there are exceptional people who are gifted with enough self-awareness to see the truth about themselves without a crisis forcing the issue. But however it happens that we finally come to realize we've been kidding ourselves by believing we have it all together, we have to come clean if we ever want the kind of life God promises us by his grace.

This doesn't mean that we're all evil or that we intentionally go around hurting other people. Our offenses come from a place of woundedness deep inside us, so they're unavoidable. And that's the point. Sin is not just about the things we do or don't do that are wrong. It's the condition in which we live, which isn't quite right.

~⌐

For a long time I thought sin was synonymous with imperfection. That was something I could relate to, because I was a perfectionist. Or maybe I should say, I was a perfectionist wanna-be.

Perfect people don't let hot oil fall on their son's head. Perfect people don't get divorced twice. Perfect people don't blow their stack at a meeting with church leaders. Perfect people don't say hurtful things to the people they love. Perfect people don't make the kinds of mistakes that I seem to make on a regular basis. I'm not perfect.

For many years, I often spent Sunday afternoon beating myself up over something I should or shouldn't have done that morning at worship. A big piece of this was the result of my insecurity, because I am a terribly self-conscious person, and I feel absolutely vulnerable when I'm standing behind the altar. Whenever I messed up, I just knew they were all thinking about what an idiot I was. The worst part was that I couldn't run and hide. So I'd push on to the benediction and then rush home afterwards where I spent the rest of the day wallowing in self-loathing.

My wallowing wasn't all about my insecurity. It was also about the need I have to be perfect. I don't know where that comes from, but I suspect it has something to do with a deep feeling of unworthiness, or maybe even just plain worthlessness.

Life is never easy for a perfectionist who is far from perfect. I can waste untold energy beating myself up, which is no way to live. Knowing that, I've worked hard to forgive myself for being imperfect. I've even grown to love my imperfections. They are, after all, signs of my humanity.

Learning about the role of imperfection in Native American beadwork has helped me put my perfectionism in perspective. In the midst of intricate patterns and colors, there is the tradition of an artist intentionally putting one bead out of place. The idea is that no one is perfect but God, so the out-of-place bead is an act of humility to give honor to God. This concept is so liberating for me.

Now, whenever I flub in a worship service, I say to myself, "Well, that was my bead out of place." Sometimes there are several beads out of place. Oh well. They always remind me that I'm not God and that's as it should be.

I've come to see that imperfection is not synonymous with sin. It's my inability to accept my imperfection that is sin. That's what has kept me from entering into an authentic relationship with the One who created me.

$\sim$

Back when I was in my 20s, my mom gave my sister and me lace tablecloths that had been crocheted by our great-great-grandma. When I got mine, I noticed that it had some stains on it, and of course, I wanted it to be *perfectly* white. So I soaked it in Clorox water.

Do you know what Clorox does to antique cotton? It isn't pretty. I ended up with an heirloom tablecloth that had giant holes in it. Dumb! Dumb! Dumb! I was furious with myself for ruining a family treasure that I could have one day passed on to my own daughter. How could I have been so stupid?

I couldn't bring myself to trash the tablecloth, so I tucked the shreds away in a box. Several years later, I pulled it out so I could see what I had done and kick myself again for being so stupid. That's when I realized that there was one large section of the tablecloth still intact. I took that section to a picture framer, who turned it into a work of art. Now I have a lovely piece of antique lace hanging on the wall in my living room.

One day as I was admiring the intricate lace, I was surprised to see that it had a glaring mistake in it. The lace circles with petals like daisies had been sewn together by joining two petals from one circle to two petals of another. On one of them I noticed that three petals had been joined together, so that on the next circle of lace only one petal could be joined.

My ancestor had messed up. She was not perfect—just like me. And yet, instead of tearing everything out and fixing her mistake, she simply compensated for it. The result was beautiful lacework with a message to a woman who came after her, a great-great-granddaughter she would never know.

What a gift! It was like a bead out of place, but it was so much more than that. It reminded me of how stupid and careless I had been with something so valuable, yes. But now this piece of lace that survived the Clorox had meaning for me. It revealed to me how I come from a long line of imperfect people, and how even imperfect people can create things of beauty. In fact, it may be the imperfections that make them so beautiful.

~

I have a lot of trouble with the second creation story in Genesis, at least the way it's usually interpreted.

I can't bring myself to believe that God created us to be sinless, then we blew it, and now we're doomed to live cursed lives. The text doesn't say that anywhere that I can see. The man and woman got into trouble because they wanted to be like God, but there is nothing in the Genesis story that tells us they were without sin prior to that. I suspect that it's because they were already sinners that they wanted to be like God, and not the fact that they wanted to be like God that made them sinners.

God created us to be the unique creatures we call humans. A big part of what it means to be human is to be a sinner. God created us this way, and as I see it, it's a gift. Because, when we come to see ourselves as sinners, we also come to see ourselves as human. We recognize: a) that we're not God and b) that we're all in this together. So, we can look on one another with compassion. There's nothing quite like recognizing our own limitations to lead us to give other people a break for theirs.

That's not to say that in our sinfulness we can't also cause untold grief to ourselves, one another, the world and God. Sin can certainly seize and imprison us. That's why forgiveness is so important. God's forgiveness frees us so that in addition to being sinners, we're also God's beloved saints.

My Lutheran faith tradition says that we're both saints and sinners *at the same time.* It's one of those paradoxes of the faith that we may have trouble wrapping our dualistic, either/or minds around. We try to separate the two. We think we're either saints or sinners at any given moment, but we can't be both at once.

It's like the cartoons where a little angel is perched on one shoulder, while a little devil is on the other shoulder, and each one is whispering in an ear, telling us what to do. From that dualistic perspective, life becomes all about ignoring the little devil and listening to the little angel, getting rid of the sinner part of us and trying to live as a saint.

This thinking leads to the notion that it's only the saint part of me that God loves, that God loves me despite the fact that I am a sinner. But that's not how it works. God doesn't love the saintly things about me and overlook the sinful things.

God sees it all: Nancy the saint and Nancy the sinner. That's who I am as a human being created by God, and God loves me—all of me.

Romans 5:7-8 says it so well: "Indeed, rarely will anyone die for a righteous person—though perhaps for a good person someone might actually dare to die. But God proves his love for us in that while we still were sinners Christ died for us."

So, yep, I'm a sinner. And I'm good with that.

Pexadition

❧

I couldn't wait to begin my life again in a whole new place with people who didn't know what a dork I'd been in high school. I was making a clean break from the past. Although it was only a three hour drive up I-75 from Hamilton, Ohio, to Bowling Green State University, that was all the distance I needed to become a whole new me.

A few weeks into my first semester, I stood in the doorway to my dorm room one afternoon and announced, "It looks like pexadition in here."

"What on earth are you talking about?" my roommate asked.

"It looks like pexadition in here."

"Pexadition? I have no idea what that means."

"You don't know what pexadition is?" How was it possible that she had lived this long and didn't know what the word *pexadition* meant?

I asked some other people in my freshman dorm, and nobody had any knowledge of the word. What was the matter with these people?

Growing up, I heard the word pexadition used on a regular basis. Most often, it came from my mom as she pronounced judgment on the way I kept my bedroom. "It looks like pexadition in here!"

Pexadition, as I understood it, meant that the place was a dump, like the slum area we had back in Hamilton, Ohio.

How was it that nobody at Bowling Green State University understood this word?

I decided to go to the source; I asked my mom.

As it turned out, pexadition was really *Peck's Addition*. It was named for a guy named Peck, who owned the land where the dump was located and where the housing projects were built for the black people who lived in my hometown. The word I was using had no meaning for anyone who didn't come from Hamilton, Ohio.

It was one of those times when I wondered if I could ever really leave my old self behind and become an all new and improved me, or would I always be lugging Nancy Kraft from Hamilton, Ohio, with me wherever I went.

~

The Apostle Paul had a past and it was impressive. In his letter to the Philippians, he pointed out how he was a better Jew than anyone. He was born of the tribe of Benjamin and circumcised according to Jewish tradition. He followed God's law to the letter. He defended the purity of his religion, even to the point of persecuting Christians. He meticulously observed everything set down in God's law book.

Was Paul bragging or just stating the facts? Well, it didn't matter because he said that, as far as he was concerned, "Everything I once had going for me is insignificant—dog dung. I've dumped it all in the trash so that I could embrace Christ and be embraced by him" (Philippians 3:7-8, from *The Message* translation).

Paul reminds me of the rich man who came to Jesus and asked what he must do to inherit eternal life. By way of background, he informed Jesus that he had followed the law perfectly his whole life. Jesus told him he needed to do one more thing. "Give everything you have to the poor and then follow me." That seemed to be too much for the rich man; he couldn't do it.

Paul boasted of his obedience to the law just as the rich man did, but Paul accomplished what the rich man couldn't. He actually did leave everything he had behind and he followed Jesus.

As impressive as his past was, Paul didn't rest on his laurels. It was all worthless, like dog poop that you scoop into a bag and throw in the trash. What mattered to Paul was "forgetting what lies behind and straining forward to what lies ahead." He pressed on "toward the goal for the upward call of God in Christ Jesus" (Philippians 3:12-14).

That's how Paul dealt with his past. It didn't become baggage that weighed him down. He let it go and moved on.

I think that Paul's main point was about letting go of what doesn't matter so you can grab onto what does, but his treatment of the past doesn't ring true for me.

We probably all know people who live in the past because that's when they were in their glory. No time will ever be as great as the night they carried the ball over the goal line at a high school football game, or when their father walked them down the aisle at their wedding. Their best days are behind them, and life since then has been on a steady decline.

On the other hand, some people live in the past because they can't let go of a painful time. They relive a childhood trauma every day, or they can't erase scenes from when they served in the war out of their mind. Baggage from the past is too much to bear and it paralyzes them.

The way Paul describes it, we have two options when it comes to dealing with our past: we either carry it with us, or we let it go. But could there be another way?

~

Ten years ago, there was a movie in the theaters called *Eternal Sunshine of the Spotless Mind*. It had a great premise. A man and a woman are in a loving relationship that lasts a couple of years. After they have a fight, the woman hires a firm that has the technology to erase all her memories of their relationship. When the man discovers what she's done, he decides to undergo the procedure, too. The past they shared is completely erased from both of their memories.

If you've ever tried to recover from an ended relationship with someone you love, this concept has a lot of appeal. The pain is so unbearable that you'd do just about anything to make it go away.

But alas, this is science fiction. In reality, we don't have the technology to erase our painful memories, while keeping the happy ones intact. Even though Paul claimed that he was leaving his past behind him, we can find other places in his writings that tell us he did anything but leave the past in the past. The truth is, no one can erase their past.

It makes me think about the grief process and how anxious other people can become when you hang onto it beyond the limits of their comfort. "Your mother died six months ago. Haven't you gotten over that yet?" They'll ask the question as if the loss of someone you love is something you can simply erase from your memory.

Anyone who's ever been through this kind of grief knows that's not the way it works. You never get over it. You don't leave that person in the past and move on. What you do is figure out how to move on while you bring them with you.

~❦~

For most of my adult life, I've had a lot of trouble returning to my hometown, and I've tried hard to understand why. Nothing traumatic happened to me in my childhood, no more than childhood itself tends to be somewhat traumatic for all of us.

I have fond memories of my life in Hamilton, Ohio. Yet, it was so long ago that sometimes I wonder if it was only a place I dreamt about. Whenever I return, it's like one of those dreams where nothing is quite the way it should be. Some of this is because I've distorted the truth in my memory, and some of it's because it's literally changed.

The railroad tracks that always held up traffic in the middle of town are gone. My shiny new elementary school is now an open field of grass. The restaurant where I hung out with my friends has been replaced with a discount store. It's disorienting because I wasn't there to see the transition. Whenever I return to Hamilton, I feel a lot like Rip Van Winkle when he was confronted by all the changes that occurred during the 20 years when he hit the snooze button one too many times after he dozed off.

I've come to realize, though, that what bothers me the most, when I return to the place of my childhood, is not the way Hamilton has changed. It's the way I've changed.

I'm no longer the skinny little kid who climbed the mulberry tree in the backyard. I'm not the girl who played her piccolo in the marching band at Taft High School. I'm not the young woman who necked with her boyfriend on the front porch. I'm an adult. I can stay out as late as I want now. I clean my room without being told. I have money in a pension plan, for God's sake. There are two amazing adults in the world who call me Mom, and I've even become a grandma. I stand in a pulpit and preach every Sunday to people who take me seriously and seem to care about what I have to say.

How does the new person I've become fit into a place where she never lived? There doesn't seem to be any connection. That's why it's so hard for me to go back home.

I've been working on this for a long time, and here's what I think I've figured out. It's not healthy to leave behind the person I once was so that I can become someone new. That's what I've tried to do. Of course, it's been unsettling. It's left me feeling unsure of who I am.

I've grown through the years. I've experienced many transformative moments, large and small. I'm not a child anymore. But I didn't toss that child aside when I moved away from Hamilton. It's been dishonest for me to pretend that I have. I brought her with me. She's not just someone I used to be. She's still very much a part of the person I am, and I can't move away from myself—not if I really want to *be* myself, my authentic self, my complete self.

I can't look at my life journey and say, that was then and this is now. Then is a part of now. There would be no person I am now without the person I was then. Yes, I've moved on from Hamilton, Ohio, but I carried the little girl from Hamilton with me.

~

Take that word, *pexadition,* for example. That word has come to mean more to me than an odd little linguistic curiosity from my hometown. It reflects an attitude about race that was a part of my native culture.

The racism I grew up with was subtle. That's what made it dangerous. I knew it wasn't nice to use the *n*-word. I was polite to the black people in my classes and liked to believe that I treated them just like everybody else, but I didn't. They weren't welcome in my inner circle of friends, I would never have considered dating one of them, and I had a special word for the place where they lived: *pexadition.*

College was very unsettling for me as a racist who didn't know she was a racist.

One semester I took a course in Black Literature. That's when I was introduced to authors like James Weldon Johnson, Maya Angelou, Ralph Ellison, James Baldwin, Gwendolyn Brooks and Nikki Giovanni.

It's also when I experienced how it felt to be *the other.*

For some reason I couldn't understand, my classmates, who all happened to be black, hated me. Now, if someone knows me and hates me, that's one thing. But all these people knew about me was the color of my skin and that was all it took.

To my way of thinking, this was totally unfair. I thought surely they'd appreciate the fact that, as a white person, I cared enough to learn about black writers, but that wasn't the case.

They clearly resented me for being in their class, and they let me know I didn't belong there.

If I ever dared to speak, they jumped all over me, so I learned to keep my mouth shut.

Near the end of the term, there was a lot of buzz about Nikki Giovanni coming to campus for a poetry reading. I decided it was an opportunity not to be missed.

It seemed that every black person on campus was there. I had never been in such company and admit that I felt a bit uncomfortable when I took my seat, looked around and saw no other white faces. I wondered if everyone in the room hated me like the students in my Black Literature class did.

Before Ms. Giovanni spoke, some music started playing and everyone rose to their feet. I joined them, although I had no idea what was happening.

Suddenly, I was surrounded by thousands of people who were singing a song I'd never heard before in my life. They all knew every single word, which they sang with conviction. The second verse, in particular, brought tears to my eyes: tears of compassion, contrition—and fear.

> *Stony the road we trod,*
> *bitter the chast'ning rod,*
> *felt in the day that hope unborn had died;*
> *yet with a steady beat,*
> *have not our weary feet,*
> *come to the place for which our parents sighed?*

We have come over a way that with tears has been watered,
we have come, treading our path through the blood of the
slaughtered,
out from the gloomy past, till now we stand at last
where the white gleam of our star is cast.[3]

This was why they hated me, I thought.

I went to class with them, but I knew nothing about their world. Until that moment, I had naïvely assumed our worlds were basically the same.

It's taken me a long time to recognize my own racism, something the students in my Black Literature class 40 years ago could see as soon as I walked in the door.

I think about the word *pexadition* now and cringe. I don't want to forget it because it's a word that first formed me before it could ever transform me.

All that's to say that, in dealing with our past, we have a third choice. We don't either carry it with us and allow it to bog us down, or let it go and move on. The third choice is to accept the past as a part of who we are, so we can learn from it and allow it to be a part of God's ongoing work of transformation in our lives.

---

3 "Lift Every Voice", James Weldon Johnson, 1861-1938. This song is in the hymnal of my denomination and it is known to many people as the Black National Anthem.

From Battlefield to Dancefloor

❦

When people ask me how I became a pastor, I find it a lot easier to give a simple answer that has nothing to do with the truth. It's a lot like when someone asks, "How are you?" and I reply, "Good," even though I may feel like crap. I suspect that most people appreciate that.

For the truth is, my call story has been unfolding for over 40 years. It's complicated, and I'm not sure how it will end. It amazes me that I still find myself standing behind an altar lifting a loaf of bread and a cup of wine before a congregation of the faithful every Sunday morning. I never thought I'd last this long, and yet, in a very real way, I'm just getting started.

Although I was ordained when I was 26, I didn't become a pastor until I was almost 53 years old. What took so long? Was it the diabolical oppression of organized religion? Sexism within a denomination that was experimenting with the first wave of women clergy graduating from Lutheran seminaries? Had some other external forces held me back?

Nope. It was none of that. It was me.

For a long time, whenever I looked in the mirror and saw myself in a clerical collar, I wondered, who does this woman think she is, impersonating a pastor?

I could never resolve the conflict between the person I was on the inside and the role I filled for my parishioners on the outside. Every time I stepped into the pulpit and pretended to know what I was talking about, I was convinced that I wasn't fooling anyone. Surely these people could see that I was a sheep in shepherd's clothing.

For some reason, they didn't seem to notice and treated me as if I were the real deal. Occasionally I believed it myself, although those moments were few and fleeting. Most of the time I felt like a fraud, and I didn't know how much longer I could continue the masquerade.

Nearly every day for 25 years, I thought about making a break for it and running from this absurd life I had chosen. But that was a big part of the problem. I never really felt like ordained ministry had been my choice.

꙳

When I was going through my crazy, mystical period as a college student, and I heard the voice of God saying, "Here I am, Nancy," I became convinced that God was calling me to become a pastor. That call was as real to me as anything ever has been. I never doubted it, but I fought it like a tomcat in a bubble bath, mainly because it made no sense to me.

I wasn't raised in a church family and entered seminary absolutely clueless. I hardly knew the difference between the Old Testament and the New Testament. I had no idea that, up until a few years before I began seminary, women weren't permitted to be ordained in my denomination. I was so far out of the loop that I didn't know the loop existed. And yet, I felt like I would end up looney-tunes if I didn't go to seminary. No matter where I went, no matter what I did, the hound of heaven wouldn't give me a moment's peace.

Calling a truce with God, I unfurled a white flag over my fortress and enrolled in a Lutheran seminary.

I was a Lutheran because back in junior high I had palled around with my two best friends who both attended confirmation classes at the Lutheran church, and for a few awkward years, I went with them. Becoming a Lutheran wasn't a conscious decision for me any more than the time my older brother Kenny was taking my picture on the dock at our summer cottage on the lake, and he kept telling me, "Back up! Back up! Back up!" until I found myself under water, gasping for air. Lutheranism was like that for me; I just fell into it.

Some people might say it was God's providence leading me, but at the time, the whole providence-of-God idea seemed to be an oversimplified explanation for something that, to me, just couldn't be that simple.

During those years when I struggled with my call so much that the process became painful, the idea of relinquishing my struggle to a higher power was appealing. If I couldn't find a solution to my spiritual conundrum, maybe I could let God do it for me. As I groped around in the dark, trying to figure out where God had hidden the light switch, I prayed that just this once God would give me a break and make it easy for me, but it never worked out that way.

I've heard people tell me that they've never married because the right person hasn't come along yet. Perhaps the reason I didn't do very well with marriage myself was because the person I married wasn't the right person for me. I suspect that a bigger part of the problem was me; I wasn't the right person to be married. We had a marriage license, I wore a ring on my finger, I even changed my name, but I just didn't feel it. When I had children, I always felt like a mother. However, with the father of my children, with the man I called my husband, I never felt like a wife.

I wonder now if my problem with feeling like a pastor might have been similar to my problem with feeling like a wife. Why had I never felt like a pastor, even though I'd been filling that role for so many years? Perhaps it was because the right congregation hadn't come along yet, but I suspect that a bigger part of the problem was me. I hadn't been the right person to be a pastor.

I had become battle-weary through the years. When my marriage to husband number one ended and I made some disastrous decisions in the aftermath (specifically, all that culminated in marrying so-called husband number two), I moved from my native Ohio to North Carolina for a fresh start at Advent Lutheran Church in the University City area of Charlotte. I worked alongside one of the true saints God has sent into my life, Pastor Dick Little. He gave me the space I needed to tend to my wounds from the past and heal.

As the years went by and I grew stronger, it felt like too much damage had been done, and I didn't have it in me to continue as a pastor. Any energy that I ever had for pastoral ministry had been spent long ago, and I couldn't imagine that it was ever going to return.

I enrolled at the University of North Carolina at Charlotte to earn a Master's degree in teaching English as a Second Language. I planned to teach adults to speak English and finally do what I had been considering for years—leave parish ministry. I announced my decision to the congregation, and I was on my way out.

It was over and I was relieved.

⁓

I can't remember exactly how I ended up interviewing at Holy Trinity Lutheran Church in Charlotte; it's all a blur to me. I was walking away from parish ministry. Both feet were out the door, and I was about to slam it behind me. The thought of serving another congregation had all the appeal to me of a colonoscopy.

But this wasn't just another congregation. This was Holy Trinity.

When I was asked if I wanted to interview with them, something inside me clicked and I could hardly breathe. It was another one of those mysterious encounters with the Holy like the one I experienced back when I was a clueless kid in college and felt the call to go to seminary.

I knew beyond a doubt that I was going to be the next pastor at Holy Trinity, even before the search committee had received my name as a candidate. The tedious interview process seemed to go on forever. I was ready to begin, and they were plodding along, afraid to make a decision.

I understood their fear because we had a lot in common, Holy Trinity and I. We were both survivors. Holy Trinity had escaped closing its doors by the skin of its teeth more than once. Most recently, the congregation had struggled through a time of transition as they made the decision to fully include gay folks in their community. After the majority of the straight members left, some gay folks moved in to take their place, but the trauma had taken its toll, and there were Sundays when fewer than 30 people gathered to worship.

Other Lutherans in Charlotte pointed to Holy Trinity as the poster child for what happens to your church if you let gay people in—you go down the tubes.

That's exactly why I felt called to be their pastor. I believed I had the gifts to help them change that. I longed for the day when other congregations in Charlotte would look at Holy Trinity, and instead of saying, "We don't want to be like Holy Trinity," they would say, "Why can't we be more like Holy Trinity?"

I was ready to get started, but the search committee was dragging its heels. They were afraid—afraid of making a mistake, afraid of calling the wrong person to be their pastor, afraid that their next pastor could very well be their last pastor.

~⁓

The time while the search committee was meticulously deliberating and I was chomping at the bit to get started was a liminal space for me—a between time when I was neither here nor there. The furniture was pushed back, the rug was rolled up, and I had nowhere I needed to be. So God and I danced.

It wasn't pretty in the beginning. A dance never is when both partners are trying to lead.

For as long as I could remember, I hadn't encountered God on the dance floor, but on the battlefield. It was Nancy versus God, and I never knew who was going to win in the end.

I wasn't sure what exactly was going on in my life. I had decided to leave parish ministry, yet here I was, convinced that I soon would be serving as the next pastor at Holy Trinity. What was that about? Was God pulling me into something against my will? Would I wake up someday in the future, with a heart full of resentment, asking, "My God, what have you done to me?"

In my head a ping-pong match was going on with dozens of balls in play. I needed quiet, I needed peace, I needed focus—I needed to stop all that blasted bouncing in my brain. So I decided to spend some time at a retreat center.

While I was there, the spiritual director said something to me that changed my life. After learning of my lifelong battle with God, she asked, "Nancy, why does everything have to be so hard? Is God's way always the hard way?" She suggested that maybe God isn't the enemy, and maybe God doesn't want to make my life miserable.

My approach to faith sounded ridiculous when I heard her describe it so plainly, yet I couldn't deny that this was the way I'd been dealing with my call to ordained ministry. Of course, I knew God wasn't the enemy. God loved me. Yes, I knew that.

Then she said something to me that blew my mind. "Maybe the God who loves you simply wants you to love him back."

I was dumbfounded. I had learned from so many saints of the Christian faith that the key to following God's will is surrendering my will to God's, and I had tried hard to do that, but it just hadn't worked that way for me. When I surrendered to God, I felt defeated. I resented it. I continued to want the same things for myself that I'd always wanted, but I felt forced to deny them. How could I ever love someone to whom I had surrendered myself like that?

Had I been wrong all these years? Was it possible that God didn't want me to surrender? It was such a foreign concept to me that I could hardly wrap my head around it. God loves me, and God wants me to love him back.

Have you ever known two married people who once vowed to love one another for the rest of their lives come to treat one another as adversaries? It happens so often, yet it makes no sense. When you love someone, you're on the same side, aren't you? That means you want what they want. If they want to watch a football game on a Sunday afternoon, you don't dig in your heels and refuse to allow it. What they want for themselves, you want for them, too. When you love someone, your will becomes the same.

So, the big question for me became: Do I love God?

If I love God, then I want what God wants. It's not a matter of doing battle with God and surrendering my will to God's will. It's about God's will becoming my will, too. That's the difference between encountering God as an adversary and engaging God as a dance partner.

This truth has changed my life. It's why I can say that although I was ordained when I was 26, I really didn't become a pastor until I was nearly 53 years old.

It took so long for the resentment in my heart to be replaced with joy. I needed to know that I could walk away before I could choose to stay. I stayed, not because I had to, but because I wanted to. I finally understood what it meant to love God enough to want what God wants for me.

In a lifetime of deaths and resurrections, some large and some small, this was a huge death and resurrection for me. It brought me a surprising new life. After all those years of impersonating a pastor, limping along in shoes that rubbed and pinched in all the wrong places, now I'm wearing shoes that fit so well I can hardly tell I'm wearing them at all.

Is that the story of how I became a pastor? Not exactly. It's the story of how I'm continuing to become a pastor. It's the story of how I'm learning to follow God's lead, and together we're creating a unique dance that I like to believe will never end.

A Multitude of
Heavenly Footprints

❧

On a Tuesday I was in court finalizing my second divorce, and then on Saturday of that same week, I loaded a Ryder truck with all my earthly possessions and moved 500 miles away to a city where I knew no one.

The losses in my life were considerable. I left my son Ben, who would be entering his senior year of high school; he understandably opted to remain in the same school, which he could do by moving in with his father. With Gretchen already away at college, my nest suddenly became empty, and I was alone for the first time in over 20 years. I moved away from dear friends who had been my support system in both the best and worst times of my life. I said goodbye to a church I loved so much that I had hoped to stay there until I retired.

Then there was the matter of my marriage ending. Even though it had been harmful to me on so many levels, I still felt a loss. The future I had envisioned would never come to pass. My whole life had been ripped away from me.

As I tried to figure out how to navigate this wilderness time of my life, I seemed to find myself more lost in the thick of it. I engaged in self-destructive behavior that only made matters worse. I hated myself and felt like I had become such a miserable failure that what I wanted most was simply to disappear from the face of the earth.

Although I had always prided myself on standing on my own two feet and solving my problems without help from anyone else, I had reached a time in my life when I realized that I couldn't do it anymore. Praying, "God, help me!" every moment of every day, I trusted that God would empower me to get my act together so that I could put all the messiness behind me and get on with my life.

As is so often the case, God answered my prayer in a way I hadn't expected. I thought it was all about God and me, but I learned that God doesn't come to me in a vacuum. God comes to me through other people. It's why God gives us the gift of community, so that we can be conduits of God's love for one another.

You may have heard the story of "Footprints in the Sand." It's all about a person who looks back on her life and sees two sets of footprints in the sand as God walked beside her. She notices that when she went through the toughest times, she sees only one set of footprints. When she questions God about it, she is informed that there is only one set of footprints because those were the times when God carried her.

What a load of crap! That's not the way it works at all.

Looking back over the worst times of my life, there were so many sets of footprints in the sand that it would be impossible to tell where one started and another stopped. They were the footprints of family members, supportive friends, an insightful therapist and a loving faith community—all people God placed in my life to help me through the toughest times. They were the answer to my desperate prayer, "God, help me!"

One set of footprints in the sand? Never!

~

Aaron arrived at Holy Trinity Lutheran Church in Charlotte at about the same time I did. Although he was a big, bulky man who towered over me, there was something fragile about him. At worship he always sat in one of the back pews with his head down. When I gave him communion and looked into his eyes, I could see that they were moist and red around the edges.

Sometimes Aaron brought his two children with him to worship, and often he was with a man named Fritz. I became well-acquainted with Fritz from his many phone calls and visits to my office. I could never figure out what Aaron saw in him. He was immature, possessive and lived with his own unique version of reality.

Aaron, who had just ended a long marriage to a woman, had finally freed himself from the charade he had been living as a straight man. Finding his way in this new life, the overwhelming longing he had for the love of a man led him to make a choice in partners that was unhealthy. I assumed that this was part of the process for him and figured he'd work through it and move on.

Eventually, Aaron decided to pull the plug on the relationship. I was relieved.

He seemed to be in a good place in his life. He was more focused on his work as a physician in family medicine, and his relationship with his children was on an even keel again. Becoming more involved at Holy Trinity, he was elected to our Congregation Council.

Suddenly, Aaron vanished. A couple of weeks passed and friends at church and work didn't hear squat from him.

I had a house blessing in my new home, which happened to be about two blocks from Aaron's place, and I invited just about everyone I knew to come for the party. When I looked out onto my front porch and saw a group of Holy Trinity members listening intently to someone, I was surprised to discover Aaron in the center of their gathering, sobbing his way through an unbelievable story.

Aaron told us about how he met a man named Thomas on the internet. Thomas came to visit him in Charlotte, and he held Aaron hostage in his own home for two weeks. He didn't share details, but he was terrified that Thomas might return.

I wondered if Aaron might be making the whole thing up, but when I looked at him, I saw a man who clearly had been traumatized. Hunched over with his arms pulled into his chest as if he were protecting himself from a blow, his hands trembled. When he spoke, his voice quivered, and his eyes darted about. He was always on guard for the one who had terrorized him to re-appear at any moment.

That day on my porch, Aaron vowed that he would never let Thomas into his life again, and as his pastor, I promised to do everything I could to support him. Aaron assured me that he was in counseling and would be calling me if he needed help.

I stopped by his house to see him after a few days, and he seemed to be hanging in there.

A couple of weeks later, another doctor at the clinic where Aaron worked, Brent, called to tell me that Aaron had gone AWOL again. Thomas was back.

That was all I needed to hear. I immediately threw on my superhero cape and flew off to rescue him. If Aaron was having trouble extricating Thomas from his life, I was there to save him.

When I rang the doorbell to his house, Aaron quietly slipped through the doorway and onto the porch. "You have to go before Thomas sees you," he whispered.

I wasn't about to whisper back. "Aaron, what are you talking about? I know you don't want him here."

"No, it's all right. Please go." I saw the terror in his eyes.

"I know you don't mean that. Why don't you come with me to my house, and we'll call the …"

Just then, Thomas appeared. I was surprised to see that he was a scrawny little guy, dwarfed by the size of Aaron. Why was Aaron so afraid of him?

Before I had time to think about it, Thomas came after me. He screamed every obscenity in the book in my face and made it very clear that this was "none of my fucking business" and I had to go.

"I'm not leaving until I hear Aaron ask me to leave," I insisted.

Aaron was in tears. "Yes, Pastor Nancy. I want you to leave."

So I walked away. Thomas continued to scream obscenities and threats at me until I turned the corner and he couldn't see me anymore.

When I got home, my phone was ringing. It was Thomas continuing his rant where he left off on the porch. I hung up on him.

I called Brent and described to him what had just transpired. As it turned out, Brent was as much a rescuer as I was. He donned a cape of his own and joined me in my determination to save Aaron from Thomas.

Brent and I pulled together a group of work and church friends. We all met at my place that evening and then converged on Aaron's house for an intervention.

When we rang the bell, no one came to the door. We knew Thomas and Aaron were inside because we could hear them. We pounded on the doors, front and back. Still no response from inside.

This crazed Brent. He was getting into the house whether Aaron let him in or not. As he fiddled with the lock on the patio slider, the door moved. He walked in and the rest of us followed him.

Aaron and Thomas were taking a bath together upstairs. I opted to remain down in the living room for that. The last thing Aaron needed was for his pastor to see him naked—his pastor who had just broken into his house.

A whole lot of ugliness ensued—yelling, screaming, crying. Eventually, the chaos gave way to calm expressions of loving concern and gentle coaxing. We physically surrounded Aaron, placed our hands on him and prayed for his well-being.

When Thomas saw that he was outnumbered, he slipped into the mode of also caring about Aaron. He joined our prayer circle and cried a few crocodile tears. Whatever.

We managed to convince Aaron that we were there because we loved him and we thought he needed help. He agreed to go with us to the hospital and admit himself for psychiatric care.

I called his parents, who lived out-of-state, and they assured me they were booking the first flight they could to Charlotte. They would be there when Aaron came home from the hospital. He was safe. He was free from Thomas.

That's what we thought, but we were wrong.

As it turned out, during the two days Aaron was in the hospital, Thomas visited him several times a day.

Aaron signed himself out, and he disappeared again.

That's when the real nightmare began.

Thomas did everything he could to destroy Aaron. He sent a bridge-burning letter to Aaron's boss at the clinic, using Aaron's name and his email account. He threatened to have Aaron's medical license revoked by concocting a bogus drug charge that he claimed would also result in Aaron's arrest. He made threats on his family and removed Aaron from all communication with the outside world. None of us knew where Aaron was, and we had no way of contacting him.

I received an email, supposedly from Aaron, in which he resigned from his church membership and stated that he wanted no further contact with anyone from Holy Trinity. Aaron hadn't written it. I knew that.

Over the next few weeks, I repeatedly sent emails to Aaron, never knowing if he read them or not. The emails were always the same. I told him that no matter what had happened, no matter what he had done, I loved him. All he had to do was pick up the phone and call me, any time of the day or night, and I would be in my car to come and get him. I always included my phone number. I don't know how many of those emails I wrote to Aaron, hoping maybe just one of them might slip through a crack in the prison wall that Thomas had built around him.

In the beginning of Aaron's captivity, I was frantic. Then, as the weeks began to pass, I continued to think about him, but my sense of urgency was replaced with grief. I was convinced that we had lost him forever.

I couldn't stop praying for him. Every Sunday during worship, the community prayed for him, as well. It started to feel like wishful thinking, and I was wondering how long we should continue naming him in our prayers of intercession, week after week, before we stopped. After four months passed, it seemed that the time had come. I was thinking about this one Tuesday morning while I was driving to work and my cell phone rang.

"Pastor Nancy, it's Aaron."

I could hardly breathe, but somehow I managed to speak. "Aaron! I can't tell you how glad I am to hear your voice. Are you all right? Where are you?"

"I'm at the police station in Blacksburg, Virginia."

"Where's Thomas?"

"I made a run for it while he was sleeping."

"Do you want me to come and get you?" Aaron was sobbing and didn't answer. "Aaron, can I come and get you?"

He choked the words out. "Yes, please."

"I'm on my way," I told him.

Now, Blacksburg is over three hours from Charlotte and I got a sick feeling inside. We'd been down this road before. What if Thomas found him and convinced him to come with him again? What if Aaron lost his courage?

Maybe I could find a pastor in the area to sit with him while he waits for me, I thought.

I remember that one pastor I knew from my campus ministry days lived in Blacksburg. When I called, his voice mail told me he was away on vacation. Rats. I didn't know any other pastors in Blacksburg.

I knew better than to call some random pastor I didn't know and ask her or him to help. I needed to find a pastor who was okay with the whole gay thing, and those were scarce. The last thing Aaron needed was some pastor to sit him down and tell him that he got what he deserved for sleeping with men.

In my denomination, there is a process congregations can go through to receive a special designation, *Reconciling in Christ*, or RIC. It's like the Good Housekeeping seal of approval for gay people. If a congregation is RIC, LGBT folks can be assured that it's a safe place for them to be open about who they are. Holy Trinity had been RIC for years, and at that time, we were the only RIC congregation in North Carolina. Such congregations were rare in the South.

I wondered, is it possible that there is a Lutheran congregation in Blacksburg that's RIC?

When I searched online, I saw that there were only two in the entire state of Virginia. One of them was in Blacksburg. Hallelujah!

Immediately, I called the number at the church. "Please be there, Pastor," I whispered. She was.

The pastor at the RIC church in Blacksburg was completely understanding and sat with Aaron in the police station. She even brought him lunch. By the time I arrived, she was gone, so I never had the opportunity to meet her, and now I can't even remember her name, but I will never forget her amazing kindness.

Aaron was a mess. He only had the clothes on his back, which looked like rags he had pulled from a dumpster. He'd always been on the beefy side, but now I could see his bones. What had happened to him?

On the way back to Charlotte, when he wasn't crying, Aaron shared bits and pieces of his story with me, including how Thomas made him sleep on the floor like a dog, and how he had been planning his escape for weeks.

After we arrived in Charlotte and I took Aaron to his home, he couldn't bring himself to go in. All the horrific things that had happened there flooded over him, and he couldn't do it.

So I brought him home with me.

Aaron stayed at my place, gradually trying to get his life back, what was left of it. He spent his days living in fear, convinced that Thomas wasn't done with him. He had no job to return to and wouldn't be able to find another one in Charlotte after all that had happened.

It became clear that he needed to relocate and start his life over again in a place where he could feel safe. So that's what he did. (Aaron made a new life for himself in another state. He moved forward with his career and met the love of his life. They were married in 2013.)

But the story wasn't over for me.

A few years later, I was at the big churchwide assembly of the Evangelical Lutheran Church in America where the decisions about the full inclusion of gays and lesbians in the church all came down. I went to an evening seminar that was led by some gay folks from around the country who were serving in ordained ministry—something that had not yet been officially approved in our denomination. During the question and answer period, a woman beside me shared the story of how her congregation had become Reconciling in Christ. She had spearheaded the effort and was extremely proud of her church.

After the session, I spoke to her and told her I appreciated what she had to say. When I looked down at her name tag, I saw she was from—Blacksburg, Virginia. And I lost it.

Through my tears, I told the woman about how her congregation's bold stand had made such a difference for Aaron. She knew nothing of his story until I shared it with her.

Now she was crying, too. We hugged like long-lost sisters. We were part of a community that had extended the arms of God to our brother Aaron and carried him when he cried out for help.

There's a story in Matthew 9 about a paralyzed man who is brought to Jesus for healing. He can't walk, so he can't get there on his own, and even if he could, he wouldn't be able to get anywhere near Jesus because of the crowd of people that surrounded him.

But the paralyzed man has four dear friends, and they carry him to the place where Jesus is. Then they lower their friend through the roof so Jesus can see him. Finally, it's because of *their* faith that Jesus heals the paralytic.

Where would he have been without his friends? No doubt, somewhere lying on a mat for the rest of his life.

Community is a gift for us as people of faith. In community, the strong look out for the weak. When we can't make it on our own, others carry us.

I had to find myself in a place where I was never going to make it without the help of others before I realized this. The Woman of Steel had to be completely robbed of her strength, so I could learn the source of my true strength.

My strength comes from God working through community. I think that may be what Jesus meant when he said, "Come to me all of you who are weary and carry heavy burdens and I will give you rest. My yoke is easy and my burden is light" (Matthew 11:28-30). God helps us bear our burdens by putting us in a community that bears them with us.

This isn't only true about times of trouble in our lives. It's also true about faith itself. None of us is 100% full of faith all the time. We waver. We're up and down. Sometimes we would stake our lives on the truth of the death and resurrection of Jesus. Other times we're filled with doubt. Sometimes we're courageous in the way we express our faith in the world. Other times we're paralyzed by fear.

In a faith community, at any given time, some of us are fearful, while others among us are faithful. The one who is faithful today may not be tomorrow, but there are always some of the faithful among us who can carry those of us who aren't. Sometimes you might be the one who is doing the carrying, and sometimes you may be the one who is being carried. In Christian community that's how it works.

There are some people I know who insist that they don't need to be part of a church to have a relationship with God. I can't imagine why anyone would want to attempt having a relationship with God outside the context of a faith community. Why would a person refuse a gift like that?

I can understand why people are turned off by the church. Certainly, there are many Christian congregations where the community does more to hurt than help its members. I admit that the church isn't perfect by a long shot. But when it's working, it's the community that carries us into the presence of Jesus.

That has certainly been true in my life. A multitude of heavenly footprints surrounds me.

Captive

❧

*I*n the TV show *Sex and the City*, when Miranda decides to give up on men, she turns to a worthy alternative—chocolate.

She begins with a half dozen chocolate éclairs from the bakery. After she finishes them off, she realizes they're not enough; she needs more. So she picks up a box of Duncan Hines and bakes herself a beautiful chocolate cake. When it's done, she cuts herself a tiny little sliver, eats it and walks away.

She returns and cuts herself another sliver. Then she walks away again. In no time, she's back once more to cut herself a third piece. This time she goes for it and serves herself a huge slice of cake. She devours it.

In an effort to restrain herself, Miranda covers the cake with aluminum foil.

Her resolve doesn't last long. Before you know it, she's back. She removes the foil and helps herself to another piece.

You can tell she's growing more and more disgusted with herself. This time she covers the cake with foil and puts it in the fridge. She leaves the kitchen but shortly returns for yet another piece of cake.

By now she's so repulsed by her own behavior that she throws the remaining cake in the trash can. That oughta do it!

Then we see her thinking the unthinkable. And she does it—she actually digs into the trash can for more cake. She's hit bottom.

Finally, Miranda takes action. She goes to the sink, grabs the dish soap, takes it to the trash can and pours it all over the cake. That's what it takes for her to be absolutely certain she won't be having any more of that sinful chocolate cake.

Paul writes in his letter to the Romans: "I do not understand my own actions. For I do not do what I want, but I do the very thing I hate." Sin has a grip over him that he can't shake. "For I do not do the good I want, but the evil I do not want is what I do" (7:15-19). His point is that he has a propensity to self-destruct despite his best efforts to do otherwise.

Now, some people might consider this bad news. If our purpose in life is to become pure and sinless, right up there with God, it's all rather hopeless. But is that why we're here?

I don't see it that way. I wish it were as easy as dumping dish soap on all our sinfulness and being done with it once and for all, never to sin again, but it's not. Miranda may have freed herself from eating any more of that chocolate cake in the trash can, but her brokenness ran deeper than that, just as it does for us.

What we're working toward is not holiness—it's wholeness. It begins by first facing the brokenness in ourselves.

~

I was enjoying the wedding reception for a couple I had just married who happened to both be the same gender. At the reception, I found myself in a setting that had become so familiar to me since coming to Holy Trinity that I hardly gave it a second thought. I was sitting at a large table with members of my church and every adult at this table was gay, with the exception of me. Most of them were also in long-term relationships; some had spent close to 30 years together.

I told them about a conversation I had with one of the grooms earlier in the day, before the ceremony. When I asked him how he was feeling, he shared with me that he was having a hard time dealing with his own homophobia. On his wedding day, he woke up and tried to imagine how it would feel for him to go public about his love for his soon-to-be husband in such a big way, and he was wondering if he would be able to do it.

I brought it up with my gay friends because I had never heard of such a thing and I wondered if it made sense to them. It did.

They talked about how they all struggle internally with their own personal homophobia. It shows up when they're in a public setting with their partner and they feel a need to refrain from any interaction that might be perceived even the slightest bit sexual. They don't dare hold hands. They don't put their arms around each other, even for a moment. They certainly don't kiss. They don't even stand close to each other.

Why? Well, basically it's because they don't want to upset anyone. They've been taught that while they may love one another, it's still a very private thing, and they don't want to put it out there in public because others may be offended by it. At least, that's how I understood what they were telling me. (I would imagine that some of this is a need for self-preservation, too, as they know of people who have been beaten and killed for such behavior.)

I had never been aware of this before. I didn't realize that even on their wedding day, a gay couple would have to fight their own personal homophobia in order to kiss the one they love in the presence of their friends and family.

It breaks my heart to think of it. I also understand that this is a problem mostly for people who are, what a younger member of our group referred to as, *old gay*. Young gay people don't tend to worry about such things, at least those living in a large city like Charlotte. The world is different for them. For the most part, they don't have to pretend to be someone other than who they are just to please the world around them.

It seems like at least half of the older gay people I know, at one time, have been in straight marriages, trying their darnedest to live as people they were never meant to be. I hope that in the next generation such a scenario will rarely occur.

When you've been taught all your life that who you are is wrong, or less than, or a disappointment, you learn to cope the only way you can. You hide who you are and pretend to be someone you're not, just to please other people.

Certainly, this is something that transgender people deal with. Society has taught them that they can't be the person everything within them tells them they are. Many will hide who they are until they can't stand it anymore. Then comes the turmoil of transitioning from living as a man or woman to the gender they've identified with for so long. All the while, they have to deal with internal messages that keep telling them the person they are is wrong, wrong, wrong.

I also think about the way it has been, and in many ways I suspect it continues to be, for African Americans in our country. Here in the South, every once in a while I still hear an older black person speaking to a white person deferentially, similar to the way I've heard slaves speak in old movies. It may sound like they're just being polite, but it seems overly polite. I don't hear white people talking to black people like that. I suspect it's a learned way of surviving in a world that finds self-assured black people threatening, and again, I notice it primarily among older African Americans. It's something that may be so ingrained in them that they don't know they're doing it. To get past it, many may have to deal with the racism within, which may be just as challenging as encountering the racism of others.

I've noticed this same sort of thing going on with myself. Despite my best efforts to overcome it, there remains a sexism within me that's hard to escape. I grew up in a world where being female meant being less than male, and a lady knew her place. As a pastor, I've overcome a lot of that, but I still find myself in situations where I'm deferring to a man, or holding back because I don't want to appear too pushy. I try to soften my words.

It's hard for me to assert my authority. During my first years of ordained ministry, I had such difficulty asking my secretary to do anything for me that I did nearly everything myself. I didn't want to appear bossy. Fortunately, I learned to get over it because I was working myself ragged.

Female preachers tend to use a lot of qualifiers in their sermons. Words and phrases like: *I guess, maybe, I think.* Instead of saying, "We need to be more like Jesus," we might say something like, "I think maybe we need to be more like Jesus." Men don't generally do this. It's a woman thing.

When I first learned of our tendency to diminish our authority by using qualifiers, I went back over some of my old sermons, and I was shocked to see how often I did it. Now, when I edit my sermons, that's one of the things I look for.

I have to be intentional about asserting my authority. I have to fight against my own personal sexism. There's something within me that's always pulling me down, telling me that I have to be gentler in my approach, softer with my words, or people won't like me. And God forbid people won't like me!

Is there anything more tragic than denying the person God created you to be in order to please other people? Lives are wasted in the process and the Creator must be insulted.

In our traditional Lutheran confession we say that "we are captive to sin and cannot free ourselves." Homophobia, racism, sexism—some of the many faces of sin. All are harmful, particularly when they become a part of who we are, even to the point of turning us against ourselves. The sinful world does a number on us and it's pert near impossible to shake ourselves free from it. Yes, we are captive.

~

The brain has pathways in it that are formed when we behave a certain way. The more a behavior is repeated, the more defined the pathway becomes.

If you've ever been walking in the woods, you've probably noticed that there are pathways between the trees. These are routes that have been traveled in the past. The more traveled the pathways are, the more beaten down, wider and easier they are to use. That's how it is for the pathways we have in our brains, too. The more we travel a certain pathway, the easier it becomes to use it.

When we're hiking in the woods, we tend to stay on the pathways that are well worn. It's easier for us to get from one place to another, and we don't have to worry about becoming lost. Our pathways in the brain are much the same for us. We tend to stay on the well-worn pathways, the ones that have worked for us in the past.

The most entrenched pathways are the ones we began traveling as children. Take our relationship pathways, for instance. We first learned how to navigate significant relationships in our lives from the relationships we had with our parents. From our parents we learned how to love, how to trust, how to protect ourselves. A pathway was formed. It's a well-worn pathway that's become easy for us to travel, so it continues to be the pathway we use for significant relationships in our lives.

When my marriage ended, I found myself facing relationship fears that I had been carrying around since I was a little girl. For the 20 years that I had been married, I lived within a bubble of security, and I felt protected from those childhood fears. When my bubble burst, suddenly I was six years old again.

In the beginning of my new-found singleness, I was determined to find a man to fill the void in my life. I kept telling myself that I wasn't a solo act, and I needed someone to share my life or it wasn't worth living.

Recruiting the right person to fill the vacancy for a man in my life became my primary occupation. I began dating on the internet and sometimes met up to five men in a single week. These meetings were brief, more like interviews than dates.

If we mutually decided to see one another again, then it became a matter of trying on the relationship like a new outfit. How did it look? Did it fit easily or did I have to refrain from breathing when I was in it? Was it comfortable? Would it wear well over the long haul? For years I did this. In the process, I met some great men and some major creeps.

Although my purpose was to find someone I could grow old with, that's not how it turned out for me. Instead, I learned something about myself that I needed to know if I was ever going to grow old *with myself.*

I discovered a pattern to my dating. When I became involved with a man who seemed interested in having a serious relationship with me, I found myself running away. When I became involved with a man who jerked my chain and kept me off balance by never being truly available to me, I dug in my heels and held on for dear life.

It took me a while to see the pattern, but eventually, I had to pay attention. Like the Apostle Paul who wrote, "I do not understand my own actions. For I do not do what I want, but I do the very thing I hate"—the very thing I wanted to do, I found it impossible to do. What was that about?

I learned that when someone I counted on to always love me withdrew that love, it turned me into a crazy woman. I would do anything I could to make them stay, to make them love me, even if the relationship was completely wrong for me. My behavior was totally irrational, but I couldn't help myself. I felt like I was going to die if I lost their love.

I had a history of being drawn to people who could never commit to me over the long haul, hoping that this time I'd be able to make them stay and hanging onto the relationship long after I should have ended it. This was true of my marriage and every relationship I'd had with a man since. I replayed the same scenario over and over, hoping for a different outcome and doing nothing different to change it.

Here's the hard truth about myself that I had to face: I have a neediness within me that borders on crazy. It took me a long time to see that, and it's still hard for me to admit it. Really hard. In fact I can't believe I'm admitting it here.

Ironically, I hate to be around needy people. They drive me up a wall. When someone comes to the church and starts spilling their neediness all over my office, sometimes it's all I can do to restrain myself from telling them to suck it up and get over it. Really.

So, facing my own neediness has been huge for me. I resisted the possibility during decades of therapy (on and off) until it became so obvious that I had to own up to it.

Through the years, I became a master of covering my neediness up. I suspect most people saw me as a hard woman. I presented myself as a self-assured, independent person who didn't need anybody. I hid my soft underbelly from other people and even from myself. It was a way of coping that I began learning as a six-year-old child.

When my father died, it felt like I lost my mother, too. Absorbed in her own grief, she pulled herself through each day to support her family. She had a baby and a troubled teenager to contend with and little energy left for me, the one in the middle. I felt like my whole world had been jerked out from under me. I went from the security of two parents who loved and cared for me to none. I was on my own. I coped by pretending that I could make it without help from anybody. I could take care of myself.

In reality, I desperately needed someone to take care of me.

That little girl will always be a part of the adult I've become. I've carried her brokenness with me my whole life. It wasn't until I could admit my neediness and look upon that little girl with compassion, rather than contempt, that I could begin to heal.

This is a part of my journey toward wholeness. It's overwhelming and I know I can't do it on my own. I've confessed that I'm captive to sin and cannot free myself. I've been honest about my need for God's help. And I've come to experience healing in a very real way so that I can move toward becoming the person God created me to be.

On a good day, that is. On a really good day.

~

We all have pathways in our brains. The longer we're around, the more entrenched those pathways become. Some of those pathways are helpful for us and some aren't. If you've seen a pattern in your behavior that isn't healthy, even if you've done the intensive work of understanding why you've engaged in this unhealthy behavior, it's still really hard to act differently because you're naturally drawn to the pathway that's well-traveled.

If you want to change your behavior, it means stepping off a well-established pathway and creating a new one. Can you see why that's so challenging? Changing means setting out on a different course than the one you've always used in the past. It's not well-marked and it's not easily traversed.

A new path isn't a path at all until it's been traveled a few times. It takes more than one journey to forge it, and it's challenging. There are boulders to move along the way, weeds to be chopped down and trees you may need to go around. It can be so difficult that you may return to the old path by default.

But the same old path will never get you anywhere but the same old place. There is only one way to find yourself in a new place.

Brian McLaren writes: "Faith is stepping off the map of what's known and making a new road by walking into the unknown. It's responding to God's call to adventure, stepping out on a quest for goodness, trusting that the status quo isn't as good as it gets, believing a promise that a better life is possible."[4]

That's what the life of faith looks like. It looks like "making a new road by walking into the unknown."

God gives us all opportunities to forge new pathways in our lives. We may be captive to sin, unable to free ourselves, but

---

4 *We Make the Road by Walking: A Year-long Quest for Spiritual Formation, Reorientation, and Activation.* (Jericho Books, 2014)

by the grace of God we're free. The path we travel hasn't been pre-determined. Before us is an open field yielding only to the bright sky with no landmarks in sight.

God Glimpses

❦

"What makes you think there really is a God?"

This was the logical question for Kim to ask. Raised in a conservative church and steeped in Biblical literalism, now that her critical mind had been awakened, the fortress she had constructed to contain her faith was crumbling. If she could no longer believe what she had been taught about the Bible, how could she believe in God, who, for her, had always been somewhat synonymous with the Bible?

She had asked me to meet her for coffee. For someone who doesn't drink coffee, I find myself meeting people for coffee quite a bit these days. It's a comfortable venue for younger adults, so I'm glad to meet them on their own turf.

I've come to expect that meeting a young adult for coffee means I'm in for some serious brain pickin'. They'll sit across from me, gently stroking their coffee cups with their fingers, while they grill me with the questions that have them tossing and turning at 3 AM.

Basically, they are the same questions that have *me* tossing and turning at 3 AM. These conversations consistently challenge me because I can't hide behind a pulpit, offer pat answers, or carelessly sprinkle theological jargon here and there when I'm meeting with someone who's sipping coffee across the table from me. I have to get real.

As I sat with Kim, I was thinking about another young woman I met for coffee and brain pickin' just a few days before. Like Kim, she wasn't a member of my congregation, and she was smart as a whip. But the woman I met with a few days prior had no faith background at all. She came to me mystified by a church culture that was so far removed from her experience. Kim was the exact opposite. She had been thoroughly indoctrinated with all the right answers.

It occurred to me that both women were blank slates so far as faith was concerned, but in different ways. One was a blank slate that had never been written upon and the other's slate, which once had been completely covered in writing, now had been erased. Both were sincere in their search, and both made me as comfortable as a bug under a magnifying glass catching the sun's laser-sharp heat.

"What makes me think there really is a God? Well, that's a good question. It depends on the day you ask me. I don't always believe in God, but I guess that's where faith comes in for me. I know God doesn't need me to believe in him. God is. I trust that even when I don't know if there is a God, God is never going to stop loving me. That's what I trust in. My feelings come and go. I can't trust them. What I believe comes and goes. But I trust that God's love is bigger than all that."

"How do you know that God loves you?" she asked me.

Now, the stock answer would have been some verse from the Bible like John 3:16: "For God so loved the world that he gave his only Son, so that everyone who believes in him may not perish but may have eternal life." But that's not how I know God loves me.

I'm one of those people who doesn't believe anything just because the Bible says so; it has to ring true to my own experience. I couldn't lie to her, so I said, "I know God loves me by the God glimpses I experience in my life. Again and again, something will happen in my life reminding me that God is loving and good and I can trust that. Often I experience it in something little, something I might easily miss. But if I'm paying attention, I experience God's love every day."

It may be heresy. I may not have been approved for ordination if I had answered in this way, but it's what I've experienced. It's the God glimpses that get my attention. That's where I start. Most of the time, God glimpses come to me through other people, and yes, that does include the people who have shared their own God glimpses with me within the pages of the Bible. However, I'm not someone who uses the Bible as a drunk uses a lamppost—more for support than illumination.[5] I find truth in the Bible when it shines light on my own life experience.

---

5   William Sloan Coffin, Credo. (Westminster, John Knox Press, 2004)

So we were sitting there in a suburban Panera at lunchtime. The table next to us was about two inches away, which meant that whoever was sitting there couldn't help but hear our conversation. Wouldn't you know that a man sat down at the next table right about the time we were talking about salvation. Apparently, our conversation disturbed him because he got up in a huff and moved to another table.

Then the conversation came around to hell. "Do you believe in hell?" Kim asked.

In the course of my response, I mentioned Rob Bell's new book that had raised the ire of so many Evangelicals. I asked if she'd read it and she hadn't. Well, I hadn't read it yet either, so I was a little sorry that I brought it up. I told her Bell seemed to have something to say about the existence of hell that had a lot of people all riled up, and she might want to check it out.

Right about then, two men sat down to eat at the vacant table next to us, and I heard one of them say, "Pastor Nancy!"

I looked over to see a young man, Brook, also not a member of my church, with whom I had enjoyed a similar coffee and brain pickin' session about a year earlier.

Remembering that he was a Rob Bell junky, I thought, this is too good to be true!

I explained to Brook how we were just talking about Bell's new book, *Love Wins*. When he said that he'd recently finished reading it, I asked if he could tell us a little about it.

Brook looked toward the man sitting across from him and explained to me that he was having a business meeting and really needed to take care of that, but if his lunch companion didn't mind, he could give us a quick summary. His business associate looked a little surprised but nodded his consent.

So, here I was, sitting with this young woman, for some reason talking about a book I'd never read, when all of a sudden this guy appeared, who may have been the only person I knew who had actually read the book at that time. Just a little weird.

After Brook finished his book report, he turned to his lunch companion and apologized. "I hope you don't mind … church stuff."

Brook took a sip of his coffee and then asked the man sitting across the table from him, "Do you have a church you go to?"

"I go to Christ Lutheran," the man replied.

I nearly fell off my chair because I knew that Brook was a member of—Christ Lutheran. The two men worked together, and they had no clue they both worshiped with the same church. (It's a large congregation with multiple worship services, so this is highly possible.)

All the *and ifs* started clicking through my brain. If I hadn't come here to meet Kim on this day. And if she hadn't asked me if I believe in hell. And if our first neighbor hadn't moved to another table. And if the second neighbor hadn't sat in that chair. And if I had never met him for coffee a year earlier and learned about his faith journey and his interest in Rob Bell. And if I hadn't remembered that and asked him to tell us about the book. And if he hadn't asked his associate if he has a church.

If none of that had ever happened, the two men never would have learned they are a part of the same faith community. Beyond weird.

I smiled at Kim. "How do I know there's a God? This is exactly what I was talking about."

~

I don't know what to make of bizarre coincidences like this, which seem to be happening more frequently in my life. They bring out the skeptic in me, but they also stir my faith.

There are some Christians who insist that there are no co-incidences, and God is behind everything that happens to us. That explanation has always seemed rather self-centered to me. When a great spot opens up for me on the ground level in the parking garage at Trader Joe's, I don't look at it as something God made happen. Surely, God has better things to do.

There are others who call this sort of thing *serendipity*. That seems too random to me. Neither explanation satisfies me.

~

Because I serve in an urban setting, I often have people stopping by the church asking for financial assistance. Rarely do I give money. I might take them to the gas station and fill their tank or give them food directly, but even that hardly ever happens. I've been burned more than once by people who are playing me, and I've grown cautious, so I'm usually quick to send them away. In as nice a way as possible, of course.

A man, his wife and their little boy showed up at my office, and they looked like they needed help. I decided before I met them that they weren't getting any money out of me.

The man had a wooden cross hanging from his neck, and he introduced himself to me as a minister. Handing me a flyer from his ministry, which serves the homeless in Charlotte, he told me about how they offer pizza in the park to hundreds of people every Wednesday.

Of course, as I listened to him speak, I was anticipating the moment when he would hit me up for some money. Was he soliciting assistance for his ministry? I continued nodding my head, thinking about how I was going to gently turn him down and send the three of them on their way. In as nice a way as possible, of course.

He finally got around to the point of his visit. He explained that his ministry had received some funding, which they expected to come that afternoon. They had been staying in a house owned by a woman who ended up losing it, so they had to move. Since then, they had been living in a hotel room.

Okay, here it comes, I thought. They want money for their hotel room.

He told me that they didn't have the money to pay for the room, and they needed it by 11:00 or they were going to get kicked out.

Yep, money for a room. It was pushing 11:00 so they needed it immediately. Of course.

But there was something about this guy. He seemed sincere, and his family did, too. I had no doubt that his ministry was legit.

For some reason unknown to me, I asked him how much he needed. The room was $43 a night. What kind of a room could you get in Charlotte for $43 a night? I didn't want to think about it. He already had $10, so he needed 33 more.

Okay, $33. This was not a large amount of money. They were not living a lavish lifestyle, and they were doing good in the community.

I heard a voice in my office say the words, "Let me see what I can do." Where did that come from? To my surprise, I realized that it came from me.

He told me that if I wanted to call the hotel and use a credit card, that would work. He pulled out proof of his bill. His wife offered to come back in the afternoon and return the money after they had received their funding. But really, $33?

I dug into my purse and pulled out my wallet. "Let's see how much I have here."

I started pulling out bills and counting them. I had a twenty and a five and then a bunch of ones. One, two, three, four, five, six, seven—eight.

"You aren't going to believe how much money I have in my wallet," I told them. "Exactly $33."

His eyes filled with tears. Her eyes filled with tears. Mine did, too. I felt a chill going up my spine. Oh, my! Of course, the money was theirs.

A coincidence? Serendipity? I really don't know what to do with stuff like this.

~

Not too long ago, I experienced one of the spookiest string of *and ifs* in my life. All those and-ifs converged and resulted in a new congregation at Holy Trinity that included over 50 people from the Episcopal congregation a couple of miles away from us.

I only knew about the closing of St. Andrew's Episcopal Church because a few months earlier I had moved into the Charlotte neighborhood of Merry Oaks where St. Andrew's was located.

The first week in June, in a neighborhood group email, I learned about St. Andrew's closing, and how members were planning to meet on the church lawn the next Sunday to worship together.

If I hadn't recently moved to that neighborhood, and if Austin, who also lived in Merry Oaks and attended St. Andrew's, had not sent that email to her neighbors, I would have known nothing about St. Andrew's closing and their prayer service on the lawn.

And if I hadn't gone to Letty's Restaurant for lunch that Sunday after worship.

And if I hadn't looked at how busy they were in the restaurant and decided to leave.

And if I hadn't glanced into the dining room as I was exiting and seen two friends, Jeff and Judy, sitting there. (And if I hadn't been a regular at the local contra-dance on Monday evenings, I wouldn't have known them.)

And if Jeff and Judy had been seated at any other part of the table, I would have missed them as I looked through the doorway.

And if—when I stopped by to greet Jeff and Judy—if it hadn't dawned on me that they worshiped at St. Andrew's, and if I hadn't suddenly remembered that neighborhood email, I would not have looked around the table and realized—oh my gosh, these must be people who were worshiping on the lawn today!

And if they all hadn't decided to go out to eat at Letty's Restaurant that day.

And if my compassion hadn't overridden my hunger at that moment, and if I hadn't taken the time to engage them in a conversation in which they shared their grief with me.

And if I hadn't invited them to worship with us at Holy Trinity. (Really, I was just being nice. I didn't expect them to actually come to a Lutheran church. After all, these were lifelong, Book of Common Prayer-totin' Episcopalians.)

And if, when they asked me if they could receive communion together when they came to Holy Trinity—if I hadn't been able to say yes. If we weren't a faith community that gathers around the Lord's Table every week. And if we didn't make it our practice to welcome everyone and anyone to that Table.

And if a group of them hadn't decided to show up together at Holy Trinity the next Sunday.

And if the people of Holy Trinity hadn't been so welcoming and loving.

And if our music hadn't been so vibrant and joyful, largely due to the gifts of our director of music, Ron Ellis, who had begun his ministry with us just two months before.

And if our new friends hadn't gone and told more of their friends about this little Lutheran church in the Plaza-Midwood neighborhood of Charlotte.

Well, that's a lot of and ifs. Behind each of those and ifs, there are hundreds of others that all came together.

What do I do with all those and ifs? I'm not cuckoo for Cocoa Puffs—caught in magical thinking about supernatural powers that make unnatural things happen in the world. I'm not comfortable saying God makes these things happen, but I also can't bring my skeptical self to believe that God doesn't make them happen either.

I've decided to think of them as God glimpses. Whether God made these things come about, or they just randomly happened, *I see God* in these moments.

I know I may be attaching meaning to events that would appear meaningless to someone else. I think that may be part of what it means to live a life of faith. Because I'm in relationship with God, my eyes are attuned to God glimpses, and I have the opportunity to attach meaning to the events in my life that I might otherwise miss.

I Was Wrong

❦

Megan knelt at the communion rail with her toddler, Daniel, beside her. I placed the bread in her hand. "The body of Christ, given for you," I said, and then I blessed Daniel. As I moved on, I watched out of the corner of my eye while Megan broke the bread and gave a little piece of it to her son.

I stopped in my tracks and returned to her. She was still kneeling at the rail when I leaned down and whispered in her ear with a tone of righteous indignation, "We don't allow that in the Lutheran Church."

That was the last time Megan ever worshiped with us.

I was 20-something years old and had just graduated from seminary, where I learned the rules about what was and wasn't done in the Lutheran church—rules like the one that said no one could commune before fifth grade, and they had to go through a class first.

Those who know me now would be shocked to hear that I could have done such a thing. These days I'm almost militant about everybody being welcome at the Lord's Supper—no matter who they are, what they've done, what their age—no questions asked, no one is turned away.

What happened? Well, the short story is that when I was younger I put doing the right thing above doing the loving thing. And those were the rules, doggone it.

But I've changed my mind. I don't care what the rules were. I should never have done that to Megan and her son. I was wrong.

We grow as human beings when we open ourselves up to the possibility that our experiences in the world around us can change us. Think about your own life. If you're an adult, do you still see the world the same way you did when you were a kid?

Sometimes we change so gradually that we hardly realize it's happening to us. Then there are those times when we experience an event so jarring to our way of thinking that we're transformed in an instant. The veil is lifted, and we wonder how we ever could have seen the world any other way. Those moments are a part of the human experience. This is the way God made us. We're all a work in progress. We grow.

Jesus was as human as we are. He grew along the way, too. His understanding evolved. His thinking expanded. Sometimes he was wrong, and he changed his mind. There is one story in the gospels that particularly stands out as evidence of this.

From there he set out and went away to the region of Tyre. He entered a house and did not want anyone to know he was there. Yet he could not escape notice, but a woman whose little daughter had an unclean spirit immediately heard about him, and she came and bowed down at his feet. Now the woman was a Gentile, of Syrophoenician origin. She begged him to cast the demon out of her daughter. He said to her, "Let the children be fed first, for it is not fair to take the children's food and throw it to the dogs." But she answered him, "Sir, even the dogs under the table eat the children's crumbs." Then he said to her, "For saying that, you may go—the demon has left your daughter." So she went home, found the child lying on the bed, and the demon gone. (Mark 7:24-30)

If the definition of a bigot is someone who is intolerant of a particular race or group of people, and if the only thing you knew about Jesus was what you read in this passage from Mark's gospel, Jesus was a bigot. That's why this is one of the most troubling stories we have about Jesus in the gospels.

Perhaps it might have been better to omit it. After all, those who gave us the gospels didn't give us every single thing that Jesus ever did or every word he spoke. They had to do some editing; they had to decide which episodes from Jesus' life would contribute to the larger story, which ones were most important. For some reason, Mark, and then later, Matthew, thought this was one of those stories about Jesus that we needed to hear. What were they thinking?

Jesus had been doing some pretty intense ministry. He'd just finished a heated debate with the scribes and the Pharisees about how to interpret the law. He challenged the way they had always seen things before. He pushed them to open their narrow minds, to admit they may have been wrong about some things. That's hard work!

Escaping the crowds for some much-needed rest, Jesus is soon discovered. One of the people who finds him is a woman. Well, not just any woman. This woman is a mother. And not just any mother. This mother is desperate. Her daughter has a demon living inside her that threatens to destroy her. We can only guess what that might have been about since we don't tend to associate illnesses with demons these days, but that's the way they were seen back in Jesus' day. There is a devastating illness attacking the little girl, either physically, or mentally, or spiritually. The mother is desperate.

She comes to Jesus for help, but he isn't very nice. "Let the children be fed first, for it is not fair to take the children's food and throw it to the dogs."

It's hard to believe Jesus could utter such words. Since this woman is a Gentile, and Jesus sees his mission exclusively to the Jews, he doesn't want to have a thing to do with her. He calls her a dog. (Now, if you're a dog lover, you may think of that as high praise, but trust me, Jesus doesn't mean it as a compliment.)

I suspect that most people would have walked away at this point thinking, if that man doesn't have time for me, I don't have time for him. However, a mother who is desperate to save her child isn't so easily discouraged.

No matter that the man just insulted and rejected her, she has a comeback: "Sir, even the dogs under the table eat the children's crumbs."

Jesus says, "For saying that, you may go—the demon has left your daughter."

Huh? It seems like a whole lot is left out between verse 28, where the woman comes back at Jesus, and verse 29, where he heals her daughter. We need a 28a, and a 28b, and a 28c. Why does Jesus suddenly change his tune?

Through the years, I've preached on this passage multiple times, and I've come at it from a variety of angles. I've explained the narrow-minded statement of Jesus, where he calls the woman a dog, as something that he was just saying for his disciples' benefit. He was playing devil's advocate so they could listen and learn something from the woman that Jesus himself already knew. I know another time I preached that Jesus said this simply to test the woman's faith, to see how she would react. At least once I preached about how Jesus was just being playful here; he was making a joke and engaging in some repartee with a woman whom he suspected could hold her own with him.

In all those interpretations, I was guilty of something that we so often do when we read stories about Jesus behaving in a way that doesn't line up with the Jesus we've created in our minds. I had already decided that the last thing Jesus could have been was a bigot. Jesus was the guy who loved everyone, especially the outcasts. Jesus never refused to help someone just because they weren't his kind of people. Jesus would never call the woman a dog who doesn't deserve to be fed. Jesus would never do that. My way of dealing with this passage was to work around it by making excuses for Jesus: he didn't really mean it, he was being ironic, he was playing, he had a good reason for saying what he did, and his motives were pure.

I'm in a different place now. I've changed my mind about Jesus. I don't need to make excuses for him. I can accept this passage for what it is. The simplest explanation for what Jesus says here is that Jesus meant what he said. Jesus was a bigot.

We have such twisted ideas about Jesus. One is that we like to believe Jesus was perfect, and by that, we usually mean Jesus never did or said anything wrong.

But when we talk about the perfection of Jesus, that's not what it means to be perfect from a Biblical perspective. It means that Jesus was complete. Jesus was at one with God. Jesus' will and God's will were the same. That's the perfection of Jesus.

It doesn't mean that Jesus never made a mistake, or that Jesus never said anything that was wrong.

Another thing we like to believe about Jesus is that he was all-knowing. From the time he was a babe in the manger, he knew all about what was going to happen to him in his life. He could have told you the names of his disciples before he could even speak, and he knew he was going to end up on a cross. How ridiculous is that?

We do everything in our power to resist recognizing the humanity of Jesus. Jesus is the Word made flesh. Not God masquerading as a human being, but God really as a human being. God incarnate. That means that not just a part of Jesus was human. We can't say that he was human in body, but not in mind. He was *all* human.

Some things that are true of the human experience had to be true for Jesus, too. As human beings, we're all products of our environment. Our social context influences the way we view the world around us. If we grow up in a world that be-lieves only *our* people are God's people, that's the way we'll see things. Jesus grew up in such a world. Like any human being, he was influenced by his environment.

This little confrontation with a Gentile mother who wouldn't take no for an answer was one of those life-changing moments for Jesus. He had considered his ministry exclusive to the Jews. Yes, he had healed the sick, touched the untouchable and reached out to those on the fringes of society, but they had all been Jews.

Jesus hadn't gone far enough. It took a desperate woman to challenge him on his bigotry. Jesus was one with God; he was not threatened by this Gentile woman's words. He was open to transformation. He could see that he had been wrong, and he changed his mind. That's the way it works for a human being who is perfect in his completeness.

So, we don't need to make excuses for Jesus. We can face the truth about his humanity and recognize that he did humanity better than anyone.

Does that mean he was never wrong? Of course not. Was he ever a bigot? Yes. He was human. And just like us, he could be too narrow in his thinking. Just like us, he needed to be jarred into expanding his mind. Just like us, once his mind was expanded, it could never again return to its original size.

∼

Among many in our present-day culture, it's become a sign of weakness to change your mind. Politicians, in particular, are ridiculed for this in the media. They're accused of waffling, or being inconsistent. I prefer to think of them as evolving and am wary of anyone whose mind became fossilized when they were 30 years old.

Although she was a long-time member of Holy Trinity, Louise hadn't been able to worship with us for decades, so I visited her regularly.

Shortly after Tim and Wayne started worshiping at Holy Trinity, I learned that they lived near Louise's home on Park Road, and I suggested that they go visit her. A friendship developed between the two of them and Louise, who was 98 at the time.

When Tim and Wayne sent out invitations to their wedding, Louise was invited. She was so excited for them that she gave them a set of her vintage dishes, and they were thrilled.

Shortly after this, I was visiting with Louise and she brought up *the boys*, as she called them. I didn't realize that I was about to receive her private confession.

It seems that when she was a young woman, just 19 years old, she went to the beauty shop, and when she got home, her sister told her that the man who had done her hair was a homosexual. As Louise told the story, her eyes filled with tears.

"And do you know what I did?" she asked me. "I went right to the sink and washed my hair!" Now the tears were streaming down her cheeks. "Oh, pastor, I'm so ashamed of myself! I washed my hair!"

98 years old! 98 freakin' years old and she confessed that she had been wrong. She changed her mind.

I knew her transformation was complete when her daughter Laura told me the story of a couple of guys who were neighbors after Louise came to live with her. The men decided to have a baby and had enlisted the help of a surrogate mother to have their child.

Laura wasn't sure about how she could explain this to Louise, who was 101 years old by then. How would her mother receive this information? How could she ever begin to understand and accept it?

After the second trimester, Laura decided it was time to break the news to Louise, so she said, "Mom, you know Sam and Franklin who live next door? They're going to have a baby."

The first words out of Louise's mouth were, "Oh, I need to find my knitting needles!"

Have you ever met someone whose brain became fossilized somewhere in childhood? It's a life wasted, and truly tragic. The whole point of the spiritual journey is transformation, which comes for us in big and small ways, even if we should live to be over a hundred years old. We change. We grow.

I'm expecting that to continue happening in my life. I pray I will always have the courage to admit, "I was wrong."

Atheists

❦

The summer before my daughter Gretchen started trying to have babies, she wanted to travel. When she asked me to join her on a bus tour that started in Phoenix and went to the Grand Canyon while winding its way up to Zion National Park, I was delighted. I had serious reservations, however, about being trapped with a group of strangers on a bus for eight days. Surely some of them were going to be annoying, and that wasn't my idea of a vacation.

The night we had our orientation meeting with the tour group, it took me all of one minute to figure out which person on the bus was going to bug the hell out of me. Her name was Marsha. She was a retired high school principal, which meant she had at least a Master's degree. I mention that because it makes the things that came out of her mouth even more unbelievable.

Marsha had no filter and blurted out whatever she was thinking. Like when we were driving through a town settled by Mormons. Every time she saw a satellite dish on the roof of a house, she shouted out, "No Mormons living there!"

How did she know that? Well, because Mormons don't have TVs, of course. Throughout the trip she continued to confuse the Mormons with the Amish.

I wanted to say, "Really? Mitt Romney and the Osmonds don't own TVs?" But I kept my mouth shut because I had decided on the first day how I was going to cope with Marsha.

I would consider her a character on a sitcom and find humor in the things she said. So, I laughed a lot, just before I turned to Gretchen and rolled my eyes. My coping mechanism worked well until one afternoon when it became impossible for me.

There was a man on our bus who was a surgeon from Chicago. He originally came from India and his name was *Ram*.

Marsha walked up to Ram and she said, "Ram. What kind of a name is that?"

"It's a Hindu name," he replied.

Marsha's eyes popped right out of their sockets. "You're a Hindu!?"

"I am," Ram said.

Marsha came back with a question that sucked the oxygen out of the air. "Have you ever thought about becoming a Christian?"

"Why would I want to do that?" Ram asked.

Everyone on the bus was tuned in to their conversation. As someone who considers herself a Christian, I was desperately searching for Marsha's on-off switch, hoping there might be a way to shut her down.

She kept going.

Here's how she answered Ram when he asked her, "Why would I want to do that?" She said, "So when you die you can go to heaven with all of us."

Yes, she really said that, and no, I didn't laugh. Nor did I look at my daughter and roll my eyes. I had to speak.

"That is not true," I said. "I'm sorry, Ram. Not every Christian thinks that way."

I just couldn't let that one go. Really? This man should consider abandoning his life-long faith and becoming a Christian? And the reason why he should do that is so when he dies he can go to heaven with all us Christians? Really?

For Ram, I suspect the thought of spending eternity with people like Marsha wasn't sounding like much of a draw.

Since I'm not overly concerned about going to heaven, it's hard for me to understand the reasoning of someone like Marsha. I know that she isn't the only Christian who thinks this way, not by a long shot.

I wonder why the idea of heaven is so important to so many Christians. Is it because we have such a fear of dying? Is it because we're so self-centered that we can't imagine a universe without us? Or is it because we have to believe that someday we're all going to pay for what we've done or not done in this life? Is the possibility of going to heaven the Great Carrot in the Sky for us as people of faith?

The Christian church has a long history of using the promise of heaven as a way to control people, usually with a special emphasis on instilling a fear of the alternative, hell. In the time of Martin Luther, fear tactics were used by the Church to collect money in exchange for get-out-of-hell-free cards called *indulgences*. The most magnificent cathedral in Rome was built on the fears of people who didn't want to go to hell.

Perhaps even more damaging has been the idea that we don't need to change anything, but we should simply accept things the way they are and trust that someday we'll all be rewarded for our trials here on earth. That was the gospel preached to slaves in the American South. They should be satisfied with their lot in life and be the best little slaves they could be because one day they'd get their pie-in-the-sky by-and-by.

When faith is so focused on the afterlife, then the task of evangelism, sharing the good news about Jesus, is motivated by a desire to help people get into heaven. I suppose that's the way Marsha saw herself in her interaction with Ram. She was doing her bit to save him from spending eternity in hell.

Compared to some, her pitch was a soft sell. We probably all know of evangelists who do everything possible to win people for Christ: persuade, pressure and even pummel them until they submit to being saved. No tactic is too extreme because, after all, these harsh methods come from a place of love—love for the poor sinners who are bound for hell if the evangelist doesn't save them.

Somewhere along the line, the Christian faith became all wrapped up in and around the idea of heaven. The history of where this comes from and how it evolved through the years is long and complicated. Very little of that history has any connection to the Scriptures. It's surprising how little the Bible actually says about heaven. Even the little it says is open to a variety of interpretations.

Our ideas about heaven aren't derived as much from what we read *in* the Bible as they are from what we read *into* the Bible.

In the Old Testament, you will be hard-pressed to find anything about it. In the New Testament, while there is mention of heaven, it is far from the central focus of Jesus' teachings or life among his early followers. If you could conclude anything from a study of the Bible, it might be that heaven is the icing on the cake, but certainly not the cake itself. And it's entirely possible to enjoy the cake without any icing at all.

~

The morning Vivian came into my office, she was visibly shaken. I could tell that something terrible had happened and I braced myself for the worst. A parade of possible scenarios raced through my head: A divorce? A death? Financial ruin? It was none of the above.

"Oh, Pastor, I don't know what to do. Scott told me he's an atheist."

For Vivian, this was a crisis. It may or may not have been a crisis for Scott, her 17 year old son. From Vivian's perspective, Scott was asking for trouble—he was going to hell. After all, doesn't the Bible say that if you want to go to heaven, you have to believe in Jesus as your Savior?

Well, not exactly. We glean a lot of this theology from John's gospel. John was big on believing, but he never says that if you don't believe in Jesus as your Savior you will go to hell. That's something we would have to imply from our own distorted perspective on what it means to be saved and what it is we're being saved from.

The fact is, the Jesus that John reveals to us isn't all that concerned about teaching people how to avoid hell; his focus is on leading them to experience life. Not just survival, but real life, life in all its fullness—what Jesus calls abundant life, or eternal life, which is something that begins now, not just someday after we stop breathing.

I don't buy into the whole heaven-is-the-goal-of-life thing that so many other Christians do. That's one reason why I don't get all that excited about atheists.

I'm not exactly certain what someone means when they tell me they're an atheist. Does it mean they aren't so sure about God? That they don't believe in the God they learned about in Sunday school? Maybe they don't buy into a God who can't be explained by science.

It seems to me that there is a spectrum of belief, and die-hard, Bible-burnin' atheists are at the opposite end of the spectrum from dyed-in-the-wool, Bible-thumpin' Christians. (It's the ones on both extreme ends of the spectrum who scare me, the ones who are so darn certain they're right and everyone else is wrong.) At what point does a person move from being a believer to being an atheist?

I'm not sure where I would place myself on the spectrum of belief. On any given day, I'm shifting from one place to another. It isn't easy to differentiate believers from nonbelievers, and I have to wonder how much it really matters. Certainly, God loves us all, no matter where we fall on the spectrum of belief.

Maybe it doesn't matter as much for God as it does for us. For me, living with an awareness of God's love is part of what it means to live life in all its fullness, the life Jesus invites us all to participate in. God's love is a source of joy in my life. For atheists, this must be like receiving an invitation to a party they have no desire to attend; the love of God isn't a source of joy for them. From my perspective, the atheist is missing out, but maybe from the perspective of the atheist, I'm the one who's missing out.

Those of us who believe in an afterlife might opt to leave all of this up to God and take comfort in the fact that someday we'll find out who was right and who was wrong. I suspect that when the time comes, it isn't going to matter a rat's ass who was right and who was wrong. God's grace is sufficient. It is now, and it always will be—for everyone—whether they believe it or not.

~

My son Ben's brain works in an unconventional way. Keeping up with him exhausts me. I often feel like Alice trying to pin down that elusive white rabbit who has her hopelessly lost in Wonderland. While I don't always understand his way of seeing the world, I do admire his creativity, and I know beyond a doubt that he can think for himself.

When I hear people these days lamenting the lack of critical thinking skills being taught in our schools, I think of Ben. No one had to teach him to be a critical thinker; he questioned everything from the moment he emerged from my womb. Challenging me at every turn, he accepted nothing at face value. Not even the rigidity of the American education system could break him, and believe me, it tried.

There is a fine line between critical thinking and stubborn defiance, and sometimes it's hard for me to be around Ben. Gretchen insists that Ben and I are alike in that way. I refuse to believe that. (Stubbornly and defiantly, of course.)

Sometimes when Ben and I get into an argument, I feel like I'm driving my car down a one-way street, and he's coming at me going the wrong direction. Despite all my warnings, he refuses to turn around and go the way he's supposed to. Instead, he insists that *I* am the one in the wrong.

Once when Ben was visiting me at Christmastime, we were taking a morning walk in the park on December 24, and I asked him if he would attend the Christmas Eve service that night at my church. For several years he had shared this time of year with Gretchen and me, and he never attended worship with us. Never.

He considered himself an atheist, so I knew what his answer would be, but I had to invite him anyway.

"Mom, you know I don't believe in that stuff," he said.

"I'm not asking you to believe it. I'm just asking you to come because I'm the pastor and I'm your mother and it would mean a lot to me to have you there with me."

I'll never forget his reply. "Mom, if you were a leader in the Nazi party and they were having a rally tonight and you were making a speech, I wouldn't go to that either."

Now, how can you argue with logic like that?

~

In my younger years, when I was oozing with creative energy, I wrote songs for kids. It was a great way to teach Bible stories. There's something about singing a story that goes beyond learning it. The story isn't just in your head; it flows through your veins and becomes a part of who you are. I wrote a number of children's musicals when Gretchen and Ben were in elementary school, so they learned my songs.

Back when Ben was 20, it was one of those years when I saw him at Thanksgiving, and then we weren't together at Christmastime. When Gretchen came to spend Christmas with me, she brought gifts from Ben with her.

Ben gave me a fuzzy turtleneck sweater that I just loved. He also gave me an audio tape—one he made himself, especially for me. Ben, who is a gifted musician, was just learning to write music back then. He had a keyboard, a guitar and a mixer, and he did some recording. I assumed the gift was a tape of some of his songs.

Later that day, when I was in the kitchen doing dishes, Gretchen said, "Why don't you put on that tape that Ben made for you, Mom?"

As I half-listened to the tape, I suddenly realized what I was hearing. Ben had taped his own arrangements of *my* songs, the ones I wrote and taught him when he was a little boy. He didn't have any of the music on paper, but he still remembered the tunes. By adding his own creative touch to them, they sounded much better than I ever remembered.

I stopped what I was doing, sat down and listened to the whole tape, while I blotted my cheeks with Kleenex. It was beyond a doubt the best gift I had ever received from anybody in my life.

I couldn't imagine how much time Ben spent on it. Hours upon hours. These silly songs he learned from me when he was a little boy—songs about Samson, the Feeding of the 5,000, the

Sermon on the Mount and Paul on the road to Damascus—
these songs, and the faith stories they told, were still a part of
him and they would be for the rest of his life.

When I tried to express what his gift meant to me, Ben
shrugged it off and said, "It was no big deal."

But we both knew it was a very big deal.

A lot of people claim to be atheists these days. Rarely do I
meet one who can convince me that's actually the case.

$\sim$

I suspect that I am as much an atheist as most of the self-
avowed atheists I know. I still wake up in the middle of the
night from time to time wondering if it's all a sham, if God is
nothing more than a delusion. And I know for a fact that the
Church is filled with people like me.

I can't tell you how many conversations I've had with
church members who confess to me that they don't know what
they believe anymore. They don't know if they believe in heav-
en. They don't know if they believe in a bodily resurrection.
They don't know if they believe God really cares. They don't
know if they believe in God at all.

Often, this crisis of belief will keep them away from worship. When they're with other people who seem to believe all
the stuff they struggle with, they feel like a fraud, like they're
pretending to be someone they aren't. I've heard this so often

from so many Christians that I wonder if it isn't the norm for people of faith.

What I want to tell people who feel like they're not getting what everyone else at worship seems to be getting is that the Church is filled with people just like them, and from time-to-time, most of us have trouble believing the stuff we think we should be believing if we're going to consider ourselves Christians. They're not alone.

I want to talk to them about the difference between belief and faith. We tend to put way too much emphasis on belief in the church. The fact is, beliefs come and go and, if you're trusting in what you believe, you're in for a bumpy ride.

If you're going to trust in something, you'd better be sure it's trust-worthy. For me, the grace of God is worthy of my trust. Even when I don't know what I believe or I don't seem to believe much of anything at all, I trust that the grace of God won't let me down. In fact, even when I don't trust the grace of God, I trust that the grace of God won't let me down, if you can follow that line of reasoning.

Faith isn't believing stuff that is so far-fetched no one in their right mind could possibly buy into it. It's not certainty. It's not having a theological explanation for all the hard questions. Faith is trusting in a relationship that transcends all that foolishness.

I've come to the conclusion that when we're living into the faith we long to have, when we're living *as if* it were true, we're not frauds at all. That's when we're authentically living in relationship with God.

On any Sunday morning, the pews in my church are filled with people who are living *as if.* They may not always believe the words we speak, but they speak them *as if* they did. They may not be convinced that Jesus is really present in the bread and wine of communion, but they receive the meal *as if* they did because that's the best they can do. It's all too much to take it in without reservations, without doubts, without questions. So they choose to live *as if.* And that's enough.

Because here's the thing about living *as if* you were a person of faith. After a while you figure out what it really means to *be* a person of faith. And you discover that you've been one all along.

Loving Not Judging

❧

*A*fter struggling for years to determine, first, *if* they would accept gays and lesbians, and then, *how* they would accept gays and lesbians, Holy Trinity Lutheran Church had worked through the gay issue and come out on the other side. What remained a big issue for most other congregations had become a complete non-issue for them. They were one of only a handful of faith communities in Charlotte that fully supported and included LGBT folks in their ministry.

But Holy Trinity's open and affirming stance came with a price. After years of declining membership, the congregation was forced to seriously consider the possibility of closing.

Through a series of intense, soul-searching discussions, congregation members decided that closing was not an option for them. They were convinced that if Holy Trinity ceased to exist, many of their members would have nowhere to go because they would not be welcome in other congregations.

Providing a church home for gay folks had become their reason for being.

That's when I arrived on the scene. I supported their mission to the gay and lesbian community, and I was determined that we were not only going to survive; we were going to thrive.

Soon after I began my ministry with them, I noticed that there was a serious problem. Although it was our intent to include *all* people in our ministry, by specifically stating that *all* included gays and lesbians, the public perception was that we were a gay church. In an effort to include one particular group of people, others were feeling particularly excluded.

We were in a strange predicament. While other churches were struggling to discern how they might welcome gay folks into their congregation, we were trying to figure out how to communicate to straight people that they too were welcome at Holy Trinity.

It was time to broaden our mission. The way I saw it, Holy Trinity's strength was including people who were seeking a place of acceptance after being burned by faith communities where they had felt judged. They came to Holy Trinity to give the Christian church another chance.

Certainly, that included those who were lesbian, gay, bisexual and transgender, but didn't it also include people who had become de-churched for a variety of other reasons: being divorced, asking too many questions, not following the rules or fitting in, you name it? Our mission at Holy Trinity was to the de-churched. We needed to show them that this is not just another judgmental church; this is a church where all are accepted and loved unconditionally.

I designed a postcard to communicate this to the neighborhood around us. On it I had pictures representing the wide diversity of people we welcomed. The caption read: "We're in the business of loving people, not judging them." I knocked on every door within a four block radius of the church and left the cards.

My friend Michael had a soft spot for our ministry. He was in marketing and offered to meet me for lunch so I could pick his brain. Of course, I jumped at the opportunity.

I showed him the card I had been distributing. "I'm trying to figure out a tag line for our church and this is as far as I've gotten, 'We're in the business of loving people, not judging them.'"

Michael took one look at it and said, "Why not just, 'Loving not Judging'?"

Ding-ding-ding-ding-ding! It was perfect. I shared it with church leadership, and they agreed. Little did any of us realize just how much those three words would change the direction of our ministry.

Not too long after we adopted "Loving not Judging" as our mission, the Congregation Council was faced with a conundrum that tested our resolve to live it out.

A person began attending Holy Trinity who was transitioning from a man to a woman, and she wanted to sing with our choir. She intended to present herself as a woman and sing the bass part with the choir. When she asked the choir director if he was okay with that, he asked the choir. The choir decided that they would let the Congregation Council decide. There was some obvious discomfort with the idea, yet no one wanted to be the one to say no.

Now, prior to this, we had been welcoming to transgender folks. Some worshiped with us regularly as a part of the congregation, but none had been front and center yet, and that seemed to be a different matter for people.

At our Congregation Council meeting, members of the Council began to share the pros and cons of having the new person join the choir. Before long, Tom, a dear member of the Council deeply committed to our mission, said, "Wait a minute, isn't our mission 'Loving not Judging'?" Other Council members nodded in agreement. "Well then, there's our answer."

And so it was. Despite the discomfort some of us were feeling about taking this step, of course she would be welcome to sing in the choir. We are loving not judging, and that's what we do. End of discussion.

～

When a faith community commits itself to "Loving not Judging"—when it dares to put such a bold statement out there that runs so contrary to our very human propensity to do the exact opposite, to judge without loving—when it dares to make such an audacious proclamation—it's setting itself up to be severely tested.

Our mission is not a statement of fact; it is a hope and a prayer. We're striving to become loving not judging, but we haven't arrived in Loving-Not-Judging Land. Sometimes we live up to our mission, and sometimes we don't, but one thing is certain: we will continue to be challenged in our capacity to love and not judge. Just when we think we've been stretched to the max by including someone in our circle of compassion we never thought we could, someone new comes along to test the limits of our love.

~

Our capacity for loving not judging has never been tested more than it was when it came time for us to respond to the news that one of our members had done something unthinkable.

Graham was not only one of my parishioners, he was also a former Lutheran pastor. He got himself into trouble while he was serving as a missionary in another country. Suffering from some personal struggles, he acted out sexually. As if that wasn't serious enough, some of the people he engaged sexually were minors.

To say that it was unsettling to hear about this is an understatement, especially since this was a man who had done some wonderful ministry through the years. The day I sat in the courtroom for his indictment, along with other members of Holy Trinity who came to show their love and support, I could hardly believe the things I was hearing. How could

Graham be the same person the prosecuting attorney was describing?

A couple of years earlier, Graham and his wife had come to my office to tell me about what he had done. I felt disgust and nausea, compassion and sorrow, all at once. They had been waiting for him to be arrested, praying the day would never come, but knowing it was inevitable.

None of the victims had filed charges against Graham. He was going to be arrested because he had been willing to face his demons head-on and was working his way through issues that had held him captive. After he hit bottom, he sought help and confessed what he had done to a counselor. That's how his transgressions became known.

When Graham was arrested, it was all over the media. Of course, the fact that he had been clergy made his crimes all the more newsworthy.

Members of Holy Trinity were divided in the way they felt about this. Some were angry, others crushed. Then there were a few sweet souls who refused to think ill of Graham and defended him, even in the face of overwhelming evidence against him, including his own confession.

I honestly didn't know where I stood, but it wasn't my job to judge Graham. That was the court's job. As the pastor to Graham and his wife, it was my job to let them know they were loved as children of God.

The day Graham was indicted, reporters and cameras surrounded the courtroom. They particularly wanted to speak with his wife. That wasn't going to happen. In an effort to protect her, I did something that I deeply regret—I spoke to the press. I should have known better.

My sound bite that he was a "good person who made a mistake" seemed to show up everywhere. It may not have been the smartest thing to say, but I said it. Taken out of context, it sounded like I was minimizing what Graham had done. That wasn't my intent, but it's certainly what I had communicated.

The reporter who really rattled me was the one who followed me from the courthouse to my car. First she asked me how I would feel if Graham had done those things to girls in the United States. I processed that one quickly, confident that I would feel the same way. The fact that these were girls in another country didn't make what he did any more or less horrific than if they had been American girls. He had repented and worked hard to turn his life around over the past three years, which was still the important factor for me as his pastor.

Then she asked me another question that's haunted me ever since. "How would you and the people in your church feel if he had done this with children in your congregation?"

I don't know how I answered her. I said something, because I felt I had to, but such a question deserves a more thoughtful answer than the one I gave her. I was relieved when that part of the interview never appeared publicly.

For days I felt like my brain was treading water, and I was afraid that if I stopped I might drown in my doubts. What does it mean to be loving not judging in a situation like this?

Certainly, loving not judging is the Jesus way of living in the world and it runs counter to the dominant culture that always insists people get what they deserve. But would Jesus show compassion for someone who had sexually molested children? Are there some sins that are so heinous they can never be forgiven? Are acts of repentance for some sinners rejected, regardless of the sincerity of the penitent?

I've grown to understand Jesus well enough to know the answer to those questions. Jesus would be loving not judging—consistently.

Now, that's not to say that the wrongs we do can just be wiped away as if they never happened. Particularly when we've done irreparable harm to other people, there are necessary consequences. I have no doubt that this is the way the world works. Maybe this is the way God works, too. I don't know. I do know that God's justice is always tempered with mercy.

Certainly, in Graham's case, I don't excuse what he did. I also don't minimize it. He was the perpetrator of some unconscionably evil deeds. He must face consequences. But that doesn't mean God will turn his back on him, so how can I?

The love of God isn't reserved for the deserving.

By offering a loving not judging response to Graham's actions, it appeared to some people that I had sided with the offender. This was especially hurtful for those who've been victims of clergy sexual abuse. After I appeared on the evening news, I heard from some of them. Then I knew I had some repenting of my own to do.

Typically, when a clergyperson is involved in sexual abuse, their congregation will surround them with support. Members of the congregation will talk about what a wonderful person their pastor is and how the allegations couldn't possibly be true. They will ostracize the accuser and blame her or him for whatever misconduct occurred. I remembered this only too well from the time it happened with my ex-husband.

The Church has a long, sordid history of re-victimizing victims of clergy sexual abuse. This is a grave injustice that I've always spoken against. During the media coverage of Graham's case, I was accused of doing this very thing myself. I can understand why. I'm deeply sorry for anyone I may have hurt in the process. That's the last thing I wanted to do.

I've thought a lot about the question the reporter asked me: "How would you and the people in your church feel if he had done this with children in your congregation?" Even before this incident, Holy Trinity made a concerted effort to protect our children from abuse. Background checks were requested of all our adult members, particularly those who were involved with children and youth, and knowing the importance of this, members of the congregation were more than happy to provide them, even at their own expense. Ensuring the safety of our children has long been a high priority for us. God knows how precious our children are to us, and we would do anything to protect them.

How would I feel if Graham had done this with the children of Holy Trinity? The reporter's question was a good one. I ministered to the person in our midst, who happened to be the abuser. What if those he abused were also in our midst? Is it possible to show compassion to both the abuser and the abused? I don't know if it's humanly possible, but with God, I have no doubt that's the way it works.

It's been a few years now since all of this happened, but I still struggle with the memory of it. Lest I forget, all I have to do is google my name and a blog written by my greatest critic appears. In the headline I am identified by name as one who "defends a child molester and ignores the pain and suffering of child sexual abuse victims." Every once in a while I check to see if it still pops up on Google, and there it is. I wonder if it will ever go away.

To a far lesser degree, I experienced the same thing that Graham did. There are consequences for my actions, and there are some things that no amount of repentance can erase.

The irony of me pastoring a faith community whose mission is "Loving not Judging" isn't lost on me. I'm just about the most judgmental person who ever walked the face of the earth.

I've wasted some of the best years of my life comparing, competing and condemning. Now here I am at Holy Trinity, and like it or not, I'm struggling to become more loving and less judging right along with the members of my congregation. It's a growing edge for all of us. We're figuring it out as we go.

I hope we're learning that people are not either good or bad; they're more complicated than that. People are both saint and sinner at the same time, so it isn't really our job to go around deciding who the good people are and who the bad people are. We can't begin to know what's in another person's heart.

Heck, we can't even begin to know what's good and what's bad when it comes right down to it. There isn't much we can be sure of when it comes to standing in judgment over others.

The one thing we *can* be sure of is that God's love is extended to all. Even judgmental people like us.

Biblical Bullshit

❧

*P*hil's sister, Leann, was getting married in New York. He informed her that he wouldn't be able to attend the ceremony because Leann was marrying another woman, Sue. Still, Phil wanted to join the rest of the family in New York and participate in the rehearsal dinner, the reception and all the other family times over the course of the weekend.

Leann told her brother in no uncertain terms that if he couldn't attend their wedding ceremony, she didn't want him there for any other part of the weekend.

Leann and Sue were former members of a church I had pastored, and when they asked me if I would meet with Phil, I told them I'd be glad to. I couldn't imagine Phil would agree to such a thing, and I was shocked when he called me to set up an appointment.

Phil attends a conservative Baptist congregation in Charlotte where they strongly oppose gay marriage and yet, for some reason, he was willing to speak with a pastor who supported gay marriage. It wasn't his idea, but he had agreed to do it for his sister. Would he be open to changing his mind?

Thirty seconds into our meeting I knew the answer to that question was a resounding, "Hell no!"

Before Phil appeared at my office door, I vowed to myself that I would be a good little pastor. I would listen and ask questions. I would respect Phil's beliefs. If necessary, I would gently challenge his decision in a non-threatening way. That was my plan and I stuck to it—for a while.

I asked about Phil's relationship with his sister. He told me how much he loved Leann and how close all the siblings were in their family. He also volunteered that he loved Leann's partner, Sue, like she was his own sister. He could see how happy they were together, and he supported them.

Oh, there had been that one Thanksgiving when the family was going to be together and he couldn't abide the two of them sleeping in the same bedroom, but other than that, he assured me that he had never been anything but supportive of them as a couple. I just listened without challenging his reasoning, and I was really proud of myself.

"Well then, why can't you support them at their wedding?" I asked.

"Because it goes against God's word."

"I don't understand how you can support them as a couple at all then. Wouldn't you say that's also against God's word?"

The conversation went round and round, never really getting anywhere. For him, it always came back to God's word.

Considering the fact that taking a narrow, literal interpretation of the Bible is a huge hot button for me, I showed amazing restraint.

I've gotten into more than my fair share of misunderstandings with other Christians because of differing views on the Bible. From their perspective, I suspect they can't fathom how someone like me, someone who calls herself a Christian, can say the things I do when they so blatantly contradict what the Bible says. I'm not always sure what to do about this because it seems like we're speaking a different language when it comes to the Bible. They quote Bible verses to convince me of the error in my thinking, and they might as well be speaking Urdu. It's absolutely meaningless to me. I just don't read the Bible like that.

What separates us is the way we allow the Bible to inform our lives. For many Christians, quoting the Bible is an effective way to make a point. This is the way it is, they'll tell me, because it says so right here in the Bible. It's the bumper sticker approach to Scripture: "The Bible says it. I believe it. That settles it."

Sometimes I wish it were that simple. Instead, for me, it's more like: "One version of the Bible that is commonly accepted today says it. While trying to find meaning in my life, the Biblical writers are among the sacred voices that inform me. I'm open to some of the Bible's truths for me as my journey continues to unfold." It's not as catchy as, "The Bible says it. I believe it. That settles it." And it sure won't fit onto a bumper sticker.

I could tell you some of the reasons why I'm not a Biblical literalist, but then, I'm not sure there *is* such a thing as a Biblical literalist. Even those who might be labeled as such are selective about which parts of the Bible they take literally.

What most of us probably would call a Biblical literalist is someone who looks to the Bible for definitive answers.

You don't have to turn very many pages in your Bible to see that it was never intended to be read that way. It's evident from the get-go, where we have two versions of creation in the opening chapters of Genesis. If there were one, we would be able to point to it and say, "There, that's how it happened." Instead, we have two entirely different stories describing how it happened.

If the Bible were written to give us definitive answers, we also would have one story about Jesus. Instead, we have four. When Matthew, Mark, Luke and John can't agree about the way the story unfolded, how can we say that the Bible was ever intended to give us definitive answers? Which answers would those be?

It was clear from our conversation that Phil used the Bible as a rule book. I don't think that's its purpose. Jesus certainly didn't use the Scriptures as a rule book. He often turned the law inside out and challenged what once had been accepted as truth. Much the same way, in the early Church, laws that once seemed ironclad were suddenly changed or discarded altogether. (Take the need for male converts to be circumcised, for instance.)

One of the things we can learn from the witness of the Scriptures is that part of what it means to be God's people is to be open to new ways of understanding how God is working in the world. Maybe God changes, or maybe it's just our understanding of God that changes, but clearly God is a God of transformation.

When the laws of Scripture are changed within Scripture, how can we think that those laws would suddenly become etched in stone once someone decided the Bible had been completed? Isn't the Spirit still alive and active in the world today?

For me, the Bible is not a set of instructions that tells me how to live. It's not prescriptive, but descriptive. It's a collection of writings from people who have been in relationship with God. They've written about their experiences and the meaning they've gleaned from those experiences—as people of faith. Because I'm also a person of faith who searches for meaning in my own experiences, I treasure their witness. They enrich me, encourage me and often challenge me. I also feel free to disagree with them.

I think that's how we were meant to read the Scriptures.

When I sit down with the adult Sunday school class at Holy Trinity, we get into deep discussions about what it means to live out our faith in the world today. We share with one another about how it's working for us, what meaning we're finding along the way, how we struggle. We don't always agree, but the Spirit speaks to us in those open discussions. I'm thankful to be a part of a community of faith where that can happen.

In the same way, the authors of the Scriptures are also a part of my faith community, and they speak to me. I may not always agree with what they have to say, but I trust that the Spirit is at work as they inform me along the way. Their witness has stood the test of time. They've spoken to millions of Christians throughout the centuries, and that gives them a level of credibility that makes them hard to dismiss. They're a treasure to me. I can't imagine how I would negotiate the life of faith without them. I suspect I'd be lost. And yet, the Biblical witnesses don't tell me how to live.

Does that make me a heretic? I don't think so. It just means that when I read the Bible I'm not expecting answers. I'm expecting a conversation.

As you can see, there was a lot I could have said to Phil about the Bible, but I knew I wasn't going to change his mind, so I decided to respect his Biblical interpretation and take another approach.

I would appeal to him as a brother who loves his sister.

"What do you think Jesus would do in your situation? Would Jesus go to the wedding?" I asked.

"Absolutely not."

This wasn't the answer I was expecting because, from my perspective, even a fundamentalist Christian doesn't have a Biblical basis for saying Jesus was against homosexuality. The sum total of words he spoke about homosexuality amounts to exactly zilch.

"How can you know that?" I asked.

"Because Jesus said that marriage is between a man and a woman."

Say what? I searched my mental file of Bible passages trying to figure out where he was getting such an idea until I realized what he must have been referring to. It's where Jesus was asked if it's lawful for a man to divorce his wife and he answered, "Have you not heard that the one who made them at the beginning 'made them male and female,' and said, 'For this reason a man shall leave his father and mother and be joined to his wife, and the two shall become one flesh'? Therefore what God has joined together, let no one separate" (Matthew 19:3-6).

"Are you talking about the time Jesus was answering a question about divorce?" I asked.

"Yes, that's it," Phil said. "And he says that a marriage is between a man and a woman."

"But Jesus was answering a question about divorce. He wasn't prescribing how marriages should be. He was simply describing the way marriages were in his context."

My point fell on deaf ears, and despite my best efforts not to get into a debate about what the Scriptures did or did not say, that's exactly what we were doing. This wasn't where I wanted to go with him, so I shifted gears again.

"One of the things I know about Jesus is that he always put doing the loving thing above following the rules," I told him. "It seems to me, you're saying that you're willing to put your need to be right above loving your sister. Have you thought

Biblical Bullshit

about the long-term effect this will have on your relationship with her if you don't go to the wedding?"

"Yes," he said. "But I've also thought about what I will say to God when we come face-to-face, and that's more important to me."

"Do you believe that God is a God of love and forgiveness?"

"I do."

Now I thought I was getting somewhere. I had logic on my side. "Then why wouldn't God forgive you for going to your sister's wedding, even if you believe it's wrong, if you did so out of love for your sister?"

"Because God spoke to me. After my conversation with Leann, I'd been praying about this whole thing. I opened my Bible and God gave me an answer. It was like all the words faded away, but one verse came up out of the page. It was a verse from Corinthians: 'Be steadfast, immoveable, always excelling in the work of the Lord.' I know God is telling me to stand my ground on this."

Well, that's it, I thought. He had played the God-spoke-to-me card and I couldn't win. Although I felt a need to address his interpretation, I knew it was pointless.

"And you don't think that maybe you were looking for something to reinforce what you already wanted to find?"

"Believe me, I wasn't looking for this," he explained. Somehow I doubted that.

"I can't imagine God would ever tell you not to make the loving choice. That makes no sense to me. Can you at least

154

consider the possibility that you might be wrong in your interpretation of that verse?"

He assured me that there had only been a few times in his life when God had spoken to him directly like this, and he couldn't ignore it. He had to do what God was telling him to do.

"That is such bullshit!"

Yes, in exasperation, I did what I had vowed I would not do before Phil came into my office. I told him exactly what I thought of his direct message from God.

Was I wrong? Of course, I probably could have chosen other words to make my point. But was I wrong in my assessment? That's harder to say.

Is it possible for God to speak to people by lifting words up off the pages of the Bible? I don't know. People in the Bible report hearing direct communication from God. There also have been times in my life when I've felt God speaking to me. It hasn't occurred on a daily basis, and it hasn't been like a bolt of lightning out of the sky. Yet it's happened.

Here's the problem for me. How do we know that it's God doing the talking? How did Phil know God was telling him to stick to his guns in that Bible passage that came jumping out at him? How did he know he wasn't just seeing the message that he wanted to see in those words? Is it not also possible that God sent him to talk with a very liberal pastor who would open his mind to the error of his ways? One is as probable as the other.

~⌒⌐

About a week later, I shared this story with the members of my pastors' Bible study group. They loved it, especially the part where I told Phil his interpretation of that Bible passage jumping off the page was bullshit. I stuck it to him good! It's so fun to tell my colleagues stories like that, stories where I'm clearly the hero.

But after I heard myself telling the story of my triumph out loud, I had to step back and examine my interaction with Phil again. I had been no hero. Far from it. I actually told another Christian that his deepest held beliefs are bullshit. In doing so, I put my need to prove that I'm right above doing the loving thing, which was exactly what I had accused him of doing.

That's the thing about standing in judgment of people I've decided are judgmental. As soon as I call them on it, I've become judgmental, too. I hate it when that happens!

I thought of the verses in Ephesians that describe how God's people are called to treat one another once they have a new life in Christ: "Lead a life worthy of the calling to which you have been called, with all humility and gentleness, with patience, bearing with one another in love" (4:1-2).

I have to wonder ... If I saw those words levitate off the page in my Bible, would I live them with as much conviction as Phil attached to his revelation from God, or would I conveniently dismiss them as bullshit?

Hindsight, Humor and Healing

❦

$\mathcal{A}$ picture of me on the day of my ordination sits on a shelf in my office at Holy Trinity. As I study that young woman in her mid-twenties, I try to imagine what she was thinking at that moment. It was a time of firsts for her. She had just given birth to her first born. She was anxious about her first call, serving as an associate pastor with the good people of Trinity Lutheran Church in Jamestown, North Dakota. She had a lot to work through as she figured out who she was and what it meant to be a pastor. The fact that she was a woman and had never actually observed how a woman does such a thing didn't help.

As a young pastor, I had a lot of difficulty adapting to working with a secretary. It was her job to type letters for me, make appointments for me and attend to all kinds of details on my behalf. The problem was, I couldn't bring myself to ask her.

(From what I hear, this has been a fairly common problem for other women who have an administrative assistant or secretary for the first time.)

For me, there was an additional layer to my discomfort. Our church secretary, a lovely woman named Dorothy, was about the age of my mother, who had worked the better part of her life as a secretary. As I was growing up, I often heard her tell me about how exhausted and stressed she was because of all the demands placed upon her by her boss. How could I do this to another woman?

Everything my male colleagues asked Dorothy to do for them, I did myself. Mind you, this was back in the days when we typed on stencils and used correction fluid, which I globbed on my pages liberally. We also printed on messy mimeograph machines with big tubes of ink that always ended up all over my clothes. Despite the fact that Dorothy was much more skilled at these tasks than I was, I didn't want to burden her.

After Dorothy went home in the afternoon, I took a seat behind the Selectric typewriter in her office, and my day as my own secretary was just beginning.

This went on for almost three years—until the week when I typed up a bulletin insert listing all the supplies people could save at home and bring to the church for Vacation Bible School. You know, things like margarine tub lids, oatmeal boxes, cotton balls and old shirts.

It wasn't until I was in worship on Sunday morning that I noticed my typo. *Old shirts* was missing the *r*. I held my breath, hoping nobody else saw it, and when I heard nothing, I exhaled.

Later that afternoon, I had to stop by the church. When I opened the door to Dorothy's office, I was mortified to see all the leftover bulletin inserts blanketing the room: on her desk, on the counters, on the floor. On every one, *old shits* had been circled with a red pen. I quickly gathered the papers up, took them to my office and threw them away. Whoever left them there assumed Dorothy had typed them, and the last thing I wanted was for her to feel belittled for something that I had done.

As it turned out, the senior pastor thought the mistake was hysterical, and he was the one who had spread the papers all over Dorothy's office. I couldn't let her take the blame, so I fessed up. That is the exact moment I resigned from being my own secretary.

I was humiliated. Not only had my mistake been exposed, but my failure to act like a real pastor had been revealed, as well. Although I was ordained just like my male colleagues, I was having trouble differentiating myself from the church secretary.

As I look at myself in that ordination picture on the shelf in my office, and I think about all the changes that would unfold for that young woman in the years to come, the story of the old shits comes to mind. A lesson learned the hard way, I'm thankful that it's no longer a source of humiliation in my life. Now I think about it and chuckle.

I'm not the young woman in the picture any more. I'm not worried about how I will be able to serve in a role that was so foreign to me when I was first ordained. My anxiety has disappeared, and I'm confident and competent as a pastor.

The old shit incident was but one of a long list of sometimes silly, sometimes stupid, but pretty much always embarrassing screw ups that have marked my ministry. If I hadn't learned to laugh at myself, I would have left the ministry long ago. But I have, and that's quite a victory for someone who spent way too many years taking herself far too seriously. With each passing year, I find myself laughing more.

～

Christmas Eve is always a transcendent time for me. After so many years in ministry, all the Christmases seem to melt together. Sometimes, when I stand behind the altar singing "Silent Night," looking out over a sea of candlelit faces, I see people I loved and served in Marine City, Michigan, and Jamestown, North Dakota, and Carrollton, Ohio, and Kilgore, Ohio, and Waynesburg, Ohio, and Uniontown, Ohio, and Charlotte, North Carolina. They're all there with me, along with all the Silent Nights we shared through the years.

Of all the Christmas Eves I've known as a pastor, there's one in particular that stands out for me, one I'll never forget.

It happened at Advent Lutheran Church in Uniontown, Ohio.

We had an early worship service that was geared for families with young children. It had grown in popularity through the years, along with my creativity as a preacher.

One year, two people dressed up in a donkey costume, and I had a little dialogue with them about the first Christmas. Well, it was more a dialogue with the one in the front end, but you get what I mean.

Every year when I brought the Christmas story alive for the kids, I tried to top whatever it was I had done the year before. After the talking Christmas donkey, I was squeezing my turnip-of-a-brain to come up with another idea.

In a flash of inspiration, I thought, why settle for an animal costume when we could bring a real live animal into the church?

It was pure genius. I wrote a simple dialogue between myself and a shepherd, who would retell the Christmas story while holding a little lamb.

I called a local farm and made all the arrangements. At a designated time, after worship had begun, the farmer would bring the lamb to the church parking lot, and my shepherd, Sam, would pick up the lamb and make his entrance. It was going to cost $100 for the use of the lamb, which I paid out of my own pocket as a gift to the kids.

I couldn't wait to see the excitement in their faces and knew they would remember this for the rest of their lives.

The church was packed. Candles in glass globes lined the pews. Poinsettias and lit trees decorated the chancel. It was a magical Christmas Eve.

I invited the children to come forward for the message, and they surrounded me on the steps in front of the altar as I engaged them in some friendly banter so that the shepherd could make an entrance and interrupt us.

Well, we bantered and bantered and bantered, and I didn't see the shepherd at the back of the church. Where was he? It became comical as I rambled on, and the adults realized I was expecting someone who wasn't appearing.

Finally, I saw Sam making his way down the hallway leading to the narthex. He was walking backwards and struggling. I gave him his cue, and he was still struggling to move. What on earth?

Then I saw the problem. This wasn't a sweet, little lamb. This was a full-grown, big ol' fluffy sheep, and the animal wasn't happy. He had his legs tucked up under him so that he was a giant fuzz ball on the floor—and a very heavy one at that. (I could tell by the way Sam was straining as he tried to drag the animal with the leash.)

All of a sudden, the sheep was on his feet. He and Sam started down the center aisle, and I breathed a sigh of relief, thinking everything was going to be okay. I thought wrong.

When the sheep saw the aisle candles and the people, he tried to run away. He leapt up into the air, flipped over and landed on his back. Then, scrambling to his feet, he did it again. Again and again, as Sam pulled him down the aisle, the sheep did acrobatics, and I held my breath. Each time he did this the kids squealed with delight, which made the sheep flip out even more.

I kept praying, God, please don't let that sheep break its neck and die here right in front of all these kids on Christmas Eve, and I promise I'll never do anything this stupid again.

By the time they had reached the front of the church, I don't know who was more frazzled, Sam or the sheep. Both of them had the same terrified look in their eyes.

When I launched into the dialogue we had worked on, Sam just stared at me. He couldn't speak. So I worked both sides of the story as he stood there with his mouth open, nodding every so often. It didn't matter what I said anyway. No one was listening. They were all watching the sheep to see what crazy thing he'd do next.

You probably know where this is going, because you're a lot smarter than I was. The sheep left a Christmas present for us on the rug, right there in front of God and everybody. The kids thought it was the funniest thing they had ever seen. I knew that it was time to wrap things up before he did it again. We had to get this woolly sack of poop out of church and send him back to the farm where he belonged.

Sam went to make his exit, but the sheep had other ideas. He tucked all four legs up under himself and made like a footstool—a legless footstool.

Sam slid the stubborn animal down the aisle, to the delight of all who were present. Kids were squealing, and adults were howling. Some had tears streaming down their cheeks. The only ones who failed to see the humor in this were poor, dazed Sam and me. And the sheep, of course.

It turned out to be a Christmas Eve none of those children will ever forget, but not for the reasons I had hoped. I'll never forget it either. It will probably be one of those scenes that flashes before my eyes on my deathbed.

At the time it happened, it wasn't nearly as funny to me as it was to everyone else. Why would I think that it was a good idea to bring a farm animal into church? Why did I think I had to create a sensational experience on Christmas Eve that people would be talking about for years to come? It was my Tower of Babel, a humbling lesson in hubris.

In time, the Christmas Eve sheep fiasco evolved from being a failure to a source of joy in my life. Yes, it was a crazy idea. Yes, it didn't go according to plan. Yes, some may say that it was a disaster. But for me, the memory has become one of absolute delight. That's the healing power of hindsight humor.

∼

It was like a death for me after my life fell apart and I left everyone and everything behind me in Ohio to begin again in

North Carolina. I was in such a deep pit of pain that I felt like I would never be able to climb to the top and return to the land of the living.

Carrying the heavy burden of my grief every moment of every day was exhausting. I couldn't do it anymore. All I wanted to do was cry and sleep. Well, that's not entirely true. All I wanted to do was fade away from everyone and everything, but that wasn't possible, so I cried and slept. When I slept I prayed that I wouldn't wake up, but I always did.

How long will this go on? I wondered. I wanted the pain to end and it didn't seem to be going away on its own.

It was time for me to find a therapist in Charlotte. Several people I knew recommended Dr. Miller, so I decided to make an appointment and get started.

When I met Dr. Miller at the door to his office, I could see that he was a gentle soul, advanced in years. He showed me to a comfy chair opposite his own. After some preliminary chit-chat, he asked me to tell him about my life.

I started right in. I told him about all the tragic twists my life had taken. I cried, I bit my lip, and I pressed on. I didn't want to leave anything out. I wanted him to know about all the pain I had endured.

Occasionally he said, "Yes" or "I see" or he grunted. As I spoke, he nodded, which was all I needed to feel affirmed, so I continued.

I was telling my story, with all the sordid details, and he was listening. He cared. He was going to help me live again.

About halfway into our session, I assumed Dr. Miller was nodding when his chin fell to his chest. Quickly, his head snapped up, and for a moment, I wondered if he was having trouble staying awake, but how could anyone possibly sleep during the riveting retelling of my life story?

Again his head fell forward, and slowly his eyelids closed. Perhaps he is concentrating, I thought. His eyes are closed to block out all distractions, so he can hone in on my words.

I continued to open my woundedness to him, trusting that he would receive the secrets I shared with compassion and wisdom.

And then I heard it. Snoring. He was snoring. Snoring! My life, my pain, my drama had lulled the man to sleep.

I stopped talking for a bit to see if he would notice. This was no cat nap; he was heavy with sleep.

I quietly gathered my purse and let myself out.

At the time, I was livid. How dare that man fall asleep during the story of my life! It may have been lacking in a lot of ways, but no one could say that it hadn't at least been interesting.

I had risked opening myself up to a complete stranger. I had shared thoughts and feelings I never shared with anyone, and he had taken it all in—like a double dose of Ambien.

I forgot all about that painful day in Dr. Miller's office. Then, 15 years later it came to mind one evening as I was having dinner with a friend. I told her the story, and we both laughed to the point of tears. All these years later, I find the entire episode hysterical. The man fell asleep during the story of my life. Isn't that great?

No doubt he probably had heard it all before. I wasn't that unusual after all. Every day he met with people whose lives had taken a nosedive into the crapper. People like me, who experienced excruciating grief. People so depressed they didn't think they were going to survive. It happened all the time.

Here I thought that, in the entire history of the universe, there had never been any grief like mine, but to Dr. Miller, I was just another woman telling her tale of woe—a tale that put the poor man to sleep.

The real beauty of this memory is that, in the retelling of it, it's become an entertaining story to share with my friends. I poured out my life to a therapist and he fell asleep.

I think it's just perfect. Perfect because I lived to tell the story. And perfect because my tears have been replaced with laughter. If that's not healing, I don't know what is.

~

I've come to see every laugh as a gift. Perhaps I should say, every genuine laugh. I'm not talking about laughter that comes from a place of nervousness, meanness, or an uncomfortable desire to be accepted. That laughter has little to do with humor.

The laughter I treasure is a spontaneous reaction to the humor elicited by the irony, absurdity, or incongruity of life. It's delighting in weirdness.

It's barren Sarah's uncontrollable outburst when she is told she'll bear a child after enduring a lifetime of humiliation. It's an ecstatic King David dancing buck naked down the city streets, unashamed to show his joyful adoration of God. It's the glory of God appearing as a choir of noisy angels in the sky to sleepy shepherds warming themselves by a fire. It's a frightened, confused Mary Magdalene drawn to the grave of the one she loved, seeing him again, alive, and mistaking him for the gardener. Is there anything more delightful than the weirdness of God?

There have been episodes in my life that were more tragedy than sitcom. Nothing laugh worthy was happening. Many of those experiences will never elicit laughter from me. But the very best laughter of all seems to come when I'm able to look back on an experience that was dead serious at the time, and I find humor in it. The laughter releases the pain I had been carrying. I walked into a dark valley and thought I'd never laugh again, but I lived through it, and guess what? Looking back on it now, it was actually pretty funny.

That's when laughter is truly a gift. Every laugh becomes a defiant shake of the fist at death and a celebration of resurrection.

Where Love Leads

❧

"*C*an I take your picture?" he asked. "I think you're so awesome. You're my hero!"

I had just finished walking in the Charlotte Pride Parade, an annual event in uptown Charlotte that attracts about 100,000 people who come to freely celebrate the gifts that gay, lesbian, bisexual and transgender folks bring to our community.

Actually, I did the parade twice that day. The first time through I rode in a Volkswagen convertible at the head of the parade because I had been named the Outstanding Ally by Charlotte Pride. As I sat perched on the back of the car and waved to the crowd, they went nuts.

The reason they went nuts had little to do with me. It was about what I was wearing: a long white robe with a clerical collar around my neck and a rainbow stole hanging from my shoulders. Dressed like a professional holy person, I represented something much greater than myself to the crowd that lined Tryon Street in the buckle of the Bible Belt.

I represented people of faith who were loving and accepting. I was a symbol of God's presence to all those who watched me drive by in my robe and rainbow stole. As I waved to them, it was more than a heartfelt greeting for me; I was offering a blessing of reconciliation and healing to thousands of LGBT folks who had been deeply damaged by religion.

After I completed the route in the car, I scurried back to the beginning of the parade, so I could make my way through a second time on foot alongside the people of Holy Trinity and other open and affirming congregations in Charlotte.

Again, I noticed the way people reacted when they saw me. It wasn't me they were cheering for. It was my churchy visual image and all it represented to them.

So, the young man thought I was awesome standing there in priestly garb. He told me I was his hero.

I wasn't sure how to respond to something like that from someone I had never met before. I probably should have said something gracious like, "Thank you" or "That's so sweet of you to say that," but I had to tell him the truth.

"If you really knew me, you wouldn't say that," I said.

The poor kid. He didn't know what to say. I had rained monochromatic gray on his rainbow parade.

~⌒

When colleagues tell me they admire my bravery, or lay people look to me as a champion of justice, I always want to respond the same way I did to that kid at the parade: "If you really knew me, you wouldn't say that."

Because the truth is, the only reason I've ever done anything worthwhile for people who are treated unjustly is because I've served as the pastor of Holy Trinity Lutheran Church in Charlotte, and I must confess that when I came to serve them, that was never my intent.

Don't get me wrong. I always cared about the oppressed and the marginalized. I preached about compassion for the poor. I talked about God's call to justice. I told other people they needed to speak out on behalf of those who have no power to speak for themselves. I did all that.

What I never actually did was a blessed thing about it. Social justice was something I agreed with in theory and I was bold enough to talk about it, but I wasn't bold enough to stick my neck out and do anything about it. Although I supported activists in their work, I myself was what you might call an *inactive activist*.

Before I came to serve at Holy Trinity, the congregation had a reputation at our North Carolina Lutheran Synod assemblies. This was during the time when our denomination was struggling to decide how they would allow gays and lesbians to participate in the life of the church. For years, Holy Trinity had been a lone wolf crying in the North Carolina Lutheran wilderness, nudging the rest of us toward the full inclusion of LGBT folks.

Every year, it was always Holy Trinity pushing the issue, and every year they were quickly dismissed by the assembly. I had witnessed this from a distance, while I was serving at another congregation in the synod.

During the time when I was feeling called to serve as the next pastor of Holy Trinity, I was not feeling called to put myself out there and get shot down by my colleagues as some kind of wild-eyed radical. So, I told the search committee at Holy Trinity that if that's what they were seeking in their next pastor, I wasn't the person they wanted because, "I don't do that."

It wasn't just that I didn't speak out publicly about controversial issues. I didn't go to the microphone at synod assemblies for any reason. In 25 years, I had only done it one time. That one time was a fluke; I jumped up and spoke before I had a chance to think about it, and then I had to sit down before I fainted.

"I don't do that," I told the search committee, and I meant it. They assured me that Holy Trinity had done enough speaking out in the past, and they didn't see that I needed to do that. No one expected that of their next pastor. I was relieved.

During my pre-Holy Trinity days, I sometimes wondered if I would have been involved in the great social movements of the 20th century had I lived at the right time. Would I have marched with the suffragettes? Would I have fought for Civil Rights? Would I have been arrested for protesting the War in Vietnam?

I came close to living in the time to take a stand against Vietnam, but protests were winding down by the time I got to college. I went to a few antiwar rallies. I even got all worked up over the draft, but my passion for the cause was never matched by my action. I cheered from the sidelines and had no interest in getting out there on the playing field.

I was an inactive activist. I explained that to the people of Holy Trinity, so they would know what to expect before I came to serve them.

Those who were a part of that conversation look back on it now and laugh. Because after I began serving as pastor at Holy Trinity, I spoke about the full inclusion of LGBT folks in the life of the church at every single North Carolina Synod Assembly. In the Charlotte community, I took a public stand for marriage equality, I participated in public protests and was quoted in the newspaper and interviewed on television more times than I can count.

What happened to the inactive activist? What changed me? Quite simply, love. It was impossible for me to sit idly by while others were spewing hatred about the people I loved.

I learned the difference between believing in justice and acting for justice. Justice, in theory, is about other people. Justice, in practice, is about *my* people. At Holy Trinity, men who love men and women who love women became my people. I had to stand up for my people, the people I loved.

～

For decades, Holy Trinity worked tirelessly toward the full inclusion of gays and lesbians within the Evangelical Lutheran Church in America. I honestly didn't think it would ever happen until someday after I retired, if we were lucky, but we pressed on. Then, all of sudden, we were hearing that maybe the time had come. I couldn't believe it, because among North Carolina Lutherans, it didn't look promising. I had to be reminded that there's a whole big ELCA out there beyond North Carolina.

At the 2009 Churchwide Assembly of the ELCA in Minneapolis, I held my breath and waited and watched and prayed that the Spirit of transformation might do what seemed impossible. By then, after serving Holy Trinity for four years, I had become more than a cheerleader on the sidelines. I had to go to Minneapolis to actively work with others who, like me, felt compelled to publicly advocate for change.

I was there at the moment the change happened, and it was like nothing I'd ever experienced. I remember going outside the convention center to call Tim Funk, the religion editor from *The Charlotte Observer.* As I was giving him the news, church bells started ringing from Central Lutheran Church across the street.

It felt like the end of the war to me and, in my head, I heard the words to a good old Lutheran Advent hymn, of all things:

Comfort, comfort, now my people; tell of peace! So says our God.
Comfort those who sit in darkness mourning under sorrow's load.
To God's people now proclaim that God's pardon waits for them!
Tell them that their war is over; God will reign in peace forever.[6]

For as long as I live, I will remember that exact moment. At the time, I thought no other moment would ever compare in my lifetime. But then, on a Friday in October of 2014, I learned I had been wrong about that. The words, "Tell them that their war is over" sounded in my head again. That was the day marriage equality finally became law in North Carolina.

⁓

During my time at Holy Trinity, I had performed dozens of ceremonies for same-sex couples. Through the years, we had called them a variety of things: Blessing of Rings, Commitment

---

6 Johann G. Olearious, 1636-1711; translated by Catherine Winkworth, 1827-1878

Ceremony, Holy Union, etc. Somewhere along the way, we started calling them weddings, and we used the Lutheran liturgy from our hymnal for marriage with just a few slight changes in language.

These were joyful celebrations with the faith community gathered around the couple in prayer, but they differed from other weddings where I officiated in one important way: I never signed a marriage license. We all knew that it was a marriage only in the eyes of God and settled for that because it's all we had at the time.

Back in the spring of 2012, there was a big shift in my congregation. That's when about 20% of North Carolina's voters made the decision for all of us to define marriage as something that happens between a man and a woman, period. This was already the law in our state, but Amendment One was an attempt to make sure nobody could ever come along and change that.

At Holy Trinity we worked hard against Amendment One because it was an affront to our core values as a congregation. When it passed, we were devastated. Many of the same-gender couples in my congregation gave up all hope of ever seeing a change in North Carolina during their lifetime.

At the same time, in other states, opportunities for same-gender couples to marry were becoming available. What was to prevent couples from my congregation from going elsewhere to do what they could never do in North Carolina? One by one, I watched my parishioners go out-of-state to marry. I didn't blame them for doing this, but it grieved my heart as their pastor.

Can you imagine what it would be like if we told all of our heterosexual couples that they can't be married in their home state, within the faith communities that love and support them, by the clergy who have developed a relationship with them? It's a ludicrous scenario, isn't it? People who are deeply connected with their pastors and their faith communities expect their weddings to take place within that context. And yet, for a large number of the couples in my congregation, that wasn't possible.

I saw this as a clear violation of the freedom to practice religion in a way that's consistent with our beliefs at Holy Trinity. Of course, I would never tell another pastor or congregation that they must marry same-gender couples if doing so went against their deeply held beliefs. So, why was it okay for those who disagreed with the religious beliefs of *my* faith community to decide how we may or may not practice those beliefs?

When an opportunity came for me to take a stand for marriage equality in North Carolina, I was ready. Along with a couple from my congregation, Joanne and Cathy, and other clergy colleagues and couples from around the state, I became a plaintiff in a lawsuit, *UCC v. Cooper.*

Court cases challenging marriage equality were popping up all over the country, but this one was unique because it was the only one in the nation to challenge a state's marriage laws as a violation of the First Amendment to our U.S. Constitution that guarantees religious freedom. That's why I wanted to be a part of it. In the end, it was *our* lawsuit that finally brought marriage equality to North Carolina.

I had the privilege of marrying five couples on day one of marriage equality in Charlotte: Jess and Amber, Jeanne and Judy, Margaret and Bettie, Cathy and Joanne, and Aaron and Kevin. It was about damn time! They had spent a total of 105 years together. Between them they had fourteen children, seven grandchildren and one great-grandchild. They were pictured on the front page of *The Charlotte Observer,* all in a row, kissing at the end of the ceremony.

After fighting for so long, when we were finally victorious, it seemed surreal. I know that may sound odd for people who live in places like Massachusetts or New York where marriage equality has become a nonissue. But living in the South, after you've been denied justice your whole life, you really come to believe that it's never going to happen for you. That's how it felt for many of us in North Carolina right up until the moment when there was a seismic shift in our universe.

I thought about how it might have felt for people in other times who worked and waited and hoped for justice. I imagined what it must have been like to live in slavery your whole life and learn that finally you were free, or how people may have experienced the end of World War II when the soldiers returned home to their families, or when women in this country were at long last able to go to the polls and cast their votes. October 10, 2014, gave me a memory like that.

I also felt myself standing in a long line of people of faith who have worked for justice throughout history, the kind of justice the prophet Amos spoke of when he said, "Let justice roll down like waters, and righteousness like an ever-flowing stream" (5:24).

I understood how justice rolls down like waters in a way I never had before. At the end of the day when a judge in North Carolina declared Amendment One unconstitutional, and I finally had a moment to absorb the events of the past few hours, justice was rolling down like waters from my eyes.

I will always remember those tears. Some of them were shed for dear friends who had fought so hard for this day but never lived to see it. And some were shed in thanksgiving for the many people who will never remember what I remember. All the children born in North Carolina, that day and every day that follows, will never live in the kind of world I was living in just hours before.

Within the Charlotte interfaith community that worked together for LGBT equality, in dark times, we held onto the words of Theodore Parker for hope: "The moral arc of the universe may be long, but it bends toward justice."[7] When the moral arc of the universe bent down and touched us in North Carolina, we celebrated for weeks.

---

7 Although this quote is often attributed to Martin Luther King, Jr., he borrowed it from Theodore Parker, an abolitionist minister who first spoke these words as part of a sermon in 1853.

I've been transformed by this extraordinary time in my life. Standing alongside both my faith community and my interfaith community, I actively participated in a fight against injustice. I experienced what it's like to press on, never knowing if I would live to see the victory, but hoping and trusting that God was at work, even when the evidence seemed to say nothing would ever change.

I learned firsthand that it really is true—the moral arc of the universe may be long, but it bends toward justice. And I learned that it doesn't just bend on its own. I can't sit back and wait for it to bend. It takes effort. I am a part of the bending.

I am far from a hero. I've tucked my head inside my shell for most of my life, afraid of what might happen if I stuck my neck out. Then God planted me within a little congregation in Charlotte, North Carolina, that had been fighting for justice long before I ever arrived on the scene. They taught me that I would never truly do anything that mattered for justice as long as I remained detached from those who suffer injustice.

Once I found myself in the midst of a community where I experienced those who suffered injustice as *my* people, I was compelled to act on behalf of those I love.

When it comes to seeking justice, the challenge I continue to face is not about courage. The challenge is about love.

In Jesus' parable about separating the sheep and the goats, he says, "Truly I tell you, just as you did it to one of the least of these who are *members of my family*, you did it to me" (Matthew 25:40). When I can see the hungry, the thirsty, the stranger, the naked, the sick, and the imprisoned, as members of *my own family*, as *my people*, I'm compelled to work for justice. It's not heroic. It's just what you do for the people you love.

I pray not so much that I might grow to become braver and bolder in seeking justice in the world, but that I might grow in my ability to love a wider circle of people, including people of different races, languages, religions and life experiences. May God open my heart to love them all as members of God's family, which also happens to be *my family*. For where love leads, justice follows.

Expecting to Be Surprised

※

*D*o you believe God has a plan for us? I was at a conference for professional church leaders where the speaker made a strong case for the fact that God most certainly does not. He seemed to be reacting to people who like to explain whatever happens by saying that it's all a part of God's plan.

The idea that God has a plan for each of us can be comforting when your cancer goes into remission, but it's downright disturbing when it's spread into all your vital organs. It's hard to see how the God of goodness and love could plan such a thing. If that's what it means to say that God has a plan, I would agree with our speaker.

That's why so many Christian clichés drive me up a wall. Like, "There but by the grace of God go I." It's used when we see someone who's struggling in life, and we take comfort in the fact that our lives may not be great, but at least they're not as bad as the miserable-excuse-for-a-life that poor slob is living. However, there's a problem with saying,

"There but by the grace of God go I." It begs the question, why would a God of grace decide to give you a life of ease while inflicting a life of suffering on someone else? How could the grace of God be dispensed to some but withheld from others like that?

Another cliché that drives me up a wall and onto the ceiling is, "God is good all the time." I hear this when things have gone well in a person's life. "We got the offer we wanted on the house. God is good …" Then someone else will nod in agreement and finish the thought, "… all the time. All the time, God is good."

I don't have a problem with the statement. My beef is with the times it tends to be used. I've never heard those words spoken by someone whose life has just gone down the toilet. And yet if God is good all the time, then that would include those times when we're one flush away from losing everything.

If that's the sort of thing we mean when we say that God has a plan for us, I would agree with the speaker at our conference.

He supported his position with the story from the Book of Acts where the apostles need to find a replacement for the vacancy left by Judas, and they decide to do this by saying a prayer and casting lots.

So they proposed two, Joseph called Barsabbas, who was also known as Justus, and Matthias. Then they prayed and said, "Lord, you know everyone's heart. Show us which one of these two you have chosen to take the place in this ministry and apostleship from which Judas turned aside to go to his own place." And they cast lots for them, and the lot fell on Matthias; and he was added to the eleven apostles. (Acts 1:23-26)

I suppose the speaker's point was that it's ludicrous to think God has a specific plan for us. It's all just a crap shoot.

That's where he lost me. If anything, this story from Acts seems to refute his point. As it turned out, God *did* have a plan. It didn't happen for his followers according to their timeline, nor did it happen in the way they had expected, but God chose an apostle to round out the twelve. His name was Saul. (Better known as Paul.)

I don't believe it's true that God doesn't have a plan for us. I do believe that we can't possibly presume to know what that plan is. Such presumption always gets us into trouble because we can't avoid assigning our very human way of reasoning to God.

We assume things should go a certain way based on the bias we have for whatever works best for us. This puts us in the position of judging God's performance according to how well God is meeting our expectations. We blame God when tragedy strikes, or we pat God on the back when things go well. God is so much bigger than that. As creatures, we can't presume to see the ways of creation as the Creator does. So how can we possibly presume to understand God's plan?

Of course, this also means we have to admit that we ourselves have no control over God's plan. We can't make it unfold the way we would like it to no matter how hard we try. The fact is, it will unfold despite our best efforts.

This seems to negate the whole reason why so many people pray. When prayer is something akin to making a wish upon a star, we come to God with our desires and hope that the more fervent our prayers are, the more likely they are to come true. But the purpose of prayer isn't to align God with our desires; the purpose of prayer is to align our desires with God.

In his *Small Catechism,* when Martin Luther explained the words in the Lord's Prayer, "Your will be done, on earth as in heaven," he wrote: "In fact, God's good and gracious will comes about without our prayer, but we ask in this prayer that it may also come about in and among us."[8]

This is one of the reasons why I connect with contemplative prayer as a spiritual practice. I come to God without an agenda and open myself to God's presence in my life. I have no idea what God's plan might be, but whatever it is, I want to be a part of it.

∼

I've come to the conclusion that there's one thing I can expect from God: God isn't going to do what I expect. In other words, what I can expect is to be surprised. Perhaps that sounds like

---

8 *Small Catechism of Martin Luther,* The Lord's Prayer, the third petition.

an oxymoron. After all, if you're expecting a surprise, how can you truly be surprised?

In one of my favorite episodes of the old *Dick Van Dyke Show*, it's Rob's birthday and his wife Laura has planned a surprise party for him. Unfortunately, Rob finds out about it, and the whole episode is about him looking around every corner expecting to be surprised.

When his entire birthday goes by and there's no surprise, Rob thinks maybe he's been mistaken—there isn't going to be a surprise after all.

He gets ready for bed and he's in his pajamas as he walks into the living room to turn off the light. That's when his friends jump out and surprise the bejeebers out of him. The twist is that even though he knows he's going to be surprised, he ends up being surprised after all.

The episode is entitled, "A Surprise Surprise is a Surprise," which aptly describes the way God operates in my life. I've been surprised so many times that I've come to expect it. And yet, despite the fact that I'm expecting to be surprised, somehow I continue to be surprised over and over again.

～

Perhaps one reason why I'm susceptible to surprise is that I spend a lot of time sleepwalking. My body is often in one place while my mind is in another. I can go through a whole day without realizing it.

Years ago, I frequented McDonald's. When they went from one window to two at the drive-through, it really threw me for a loop. I'd been conditioned to drive up to the window, pay, pick up my food and drive away. Then they introduced the second window. This required driving up to the first window and paying, driving up to the second window and picking up my food and then driving away.

I can't tell you how many times I drove up to the first window, paid and then drove away, neglecting to stop at the second window to pick up my food.

I'll never forget one evening in particular when my kids were little and I stopped at McDonald's to grab some food for the whole family. I got home and they were all waiting for me. It wasn't until my daughter asked, "Where's supper?" that I realized I had paid for it, but supper was still back at McDonald's.

Sometimes when my brain goes on autopilot, it almost feels like I've had a black-out. This happens a lot when I'm doing things that I've done a bazillion times before. I can't remember if I've fed the dog, or if I've put my deodorant on. Those are inconsequential things, but there are other times when it's more important.

I especially hate it when I'm not fully present in ministry. Like when I'm saying the benediction at the end of a worship service, and I can't remember doing anything else. Did I make the announcements? Did we say the Lord's Prayer? Did I take communion? It can be unsettling.

Then there are those times when God is only a passing thought, at best. You might think that would be impossible for a pastor, but it's not. I can go through an entire day of appointments and errands and forget that what I do has any connection with God. I can even forget that God is anywhere in the vicinity.

~

I well remember a beautiful spring day when I had some azalea bushes I wanted to get into the ground, but first, I had an over-due visit with Melba. She's the oldest member of our congregation and over 30 years my senior.

Although Melba has lots of physical challenges, mentally she remains at the top of her game, and the reality of her life often makes her cranky. I can't blame her for that.

That day, I just wanted to knock this visit out, so I could get on to other things. I would briefly enter the little world of her room at the retirement home and return to my larger life in no time.

We chatted about the new Pope and her flat-screen TV and the church and her pain. Then the time came to move on to the main reason for my visit.

I opened my little box of Holy Communion-to-go, placed a wafer and a tiny glass of wine on the table, and I launched into the Brief Order for Confession and Forgiveness.

I said the words I had said so many times before: "Most merciful God, we confess that we are captive to sin and cannot free ourselves …"

Let's see. I picked up four new azalea bushes; three are bright pink and the other one, I believe, is white.

"We have not loved you with our whole heart …"

Should I plant all three of the pink ones under the pine trees in the front yard, or should I plant two pink ones and one white one and then put the other pink one someplace else, or could I put the white one someplace else?

"For the sake of your Son, Jesus Christ, have mercy on us …"

Maybe I'll have to figure it out as I go. First I'll have to dig four holes and mix some Miracle Grow with the soil.

Okay, the confession was over, so we moved on to the absolution. I assured her that because of Jesus, her sins are forgiven.

I wonder if I have enough Miracle Grow to get the job done.

"As a called and ordained minister of the church of Christ, and by his authority, I declare to you the entire forgiveness of all your sins, in the name of the Father and of the Son, and of the Holy Spirit." Reflexively drawing the outline of a cross in the air, I punctuated my words in the customary way, "Amen."

I expected to hear her echo my *amen* with one of her own; that's the way it always goes.

"Thank goodness!"

Um. Wait a minute. What was that? Did she just say, "Thank goodness?" Thank goodness?

It seemed that, unlike me, she had been paying attention. She was not somewhere else. She was present in the room. She heard the words of forgiveness, and she knew they were words of life for *her.*

Thank goodness. Those two simple words jarred me from my deep sleep like a fire alarm. Thank goodness.

As I consecrated the bread and the wine and then placed them in her hands, I wasn't thinking about azalea bushes anymore.

I was thinking about how my routine visit to this dear woman of faith was anything but routine for her. This was a holy moment. Jesus was present in the bread and wine. Melba was present in our community of faith at Holy Trinity, and we were present in her. God was here.

Instead of showing up at her door like I was delivering a pizza, I should have removed my shoes in reverence for the holiness of the ground beneath my feet.

I took her hands in mine and prayed for her the way pastors are expected to pray in these situations, offering God's word of grace to someone who so desperately needs to hear it.

"Amen," I said, indicating that this will conclude the sacred portion of our program for the afternoon.

But Melba didn't release my hands. Instead, she offered a prayer of her own. This time the word of grace was for *me*. She seemed to know that I needed to hear it, too, although I doubt she realized just how desperately on this day.

Melba finished her prayer and squeezed my hands as we both said, "Amen" together.

Yes, Melba, amen. And, thank goodness.

It was one of those times when God suddenly appeared out of nowhere and shouted, "Surprise!" in my face. A sleepwalker like me needs that from time to time. But God doesn't reserve all his surprises for me. It seems to be the way he operates in general.

God never does what we would expect. God never appears in the way we would expect. God never chooses whom we would expect. God never loves the way we would expect.

∼

Jesus was not at all what Biblical experts were expecting, and that's why they didn't have a clue who he was when they saw him. We don't really have a clue what God is up to in this world either. I trust that he's loving it, but other than that, I've learned from experience that I can expect the unexpected.

Like the time I decided to leave pastoral ministry and went back to school to do something else. I was learning to teach English as a second language to adults. I was ready to make my move. I made my announcement to the congregation and was on my way out. Both feet and 9.99 of my toes were out the door. And then, out of nowhere, God called me to serve a unique little church where I never would have imagined myself.

Suddenly, I'm more into pastoral ministry than I ever have been in my life. What's that about?

We'll never know what God's plan is for us, but I suspect he has one. It's so contrary to what we might plan for ourselves that we're going to be surprised again and again along the way. It's happened to me so many times that I expect it.

Expecting to be surprised has transformed my life into an adventure to be relished rather than an ordeal to be endured. Like Rob, who wakes up on his birthday expecting a surprise party, I anticipate a surprise with every step I take because I have a God who is ever-present, ever loving me, ever waiting to derail my best laid plans and show me his even better plans.

Pulling Meaning

⁓⊗⁓

Perhaps you've had the experience of reading a parable like "The Good Samaritan" with a group of Christians and sifting through the words for nuggets of meaning.

It can be surprising to discover that not everyone reads the parable from the same perspective. Some people identify with the man who was beaten, others see themselves in the good religious folk who didn't stop to help, and there may be some who put themselves in the place of the Samaritan who cares for the nearly dead man.

In your group study you may learn that not everyone interprets the parable in the same way. Some think it's about helping your neighbor in need. Others see it as an indictment against religion. Still others think it's about justice for people who are marginalized, like the Samaritan. There are clearly multiple ways to interpret this story.

Maybe you're convinced that everyone else is missing the point and you have the definitive interpretation. But then, years later when you return to the same parable, you discover that the way you once understood it has changed completely.

That's the way meaning-making works. There is never one absolute meaning for a story, and the meaning can change over time. Whether you're pulling meaning from literature, theater, film or a friend's anecdote, a story can have multiple meanings, and the meaning you find will likely change and evolve as you change and evolve.

When the story that you're considering is *your own* story, it's different than finding meaning in a parable or someone else's story because only one person can determine what your story means *for you*. That one person is you.

If you've ever engaged in dream therapy, you may have learned that no one else can tell you what your dreams mean for you. I know there are those who interpret dreams much like a fortune teller reads tarot cards, but that's not the way dream therapy works. If you've had a dream and you believe it might have some meaning for your life, only *you* can determine what that meaning might be. Interpreting the stories of our lives works that way, too.

Each story from your life is like a stone marking the surface of the earth, large or small. The story has a beginning and an end; it is finite. The story's meaning lies in the earth beneath; its depth is infinite. The only one who can dig for the deeper meaning of your story is you.

～

You may have noticed that some of the stories from my life have been extraordinary, while others have been quite ordinary. Yet I found as much depth of meaning in struggling with the death of my father as disposing of a concrete goose. Don't miss the opportunity to explore meaning in stories that may seem inconsequential to you. Dig around a bit before you dismiss them.

When an event in your life jars you, when it strikes you as odd or ironic, or when it leaves you questioning long held beliefs, it's a story ripe for meaning.

Consider this story about a routine trip I made to the grocery store.

I was standing in the checkout line at my neighborhood Food Lion when a boy, about 10-ish, came stomping through the front doors having a hissy fit. "I don't wanna take my medicine! I won't take my medicine, and you can't make me!"

The kid was obviously out of control. "Sounds to me like he *needs* his medicine," I muttered under my breath. It was such a perfect wisecrack that I turned around to see if I might share it with the person standing behind me in line.

A man with disheveled hair, who looked like he hadn't bathed or shaved in several days, clutched the sole item he was purchasing to his chest—an over-sized, brown bottle of cheap, nasty beer. At 8:00 in the morning. How pathetic was that? He was the caricature of an alcoholic.

Here I am, surrounded by people who can't make it through the day without their drug of choice, I thought. What a sad commentary on our world.

I collected my purchases: two bottles of Diet Dr. Pepper and some mini pretzels. This was why I had to make an emergency run to Food Lion at 8:00 on a Saturday morning.

I had carved out the day for writing. It's grueling work, and I knew I would never get through it without lots of caffeine, which I take cold, and something crunchy to eat. Yes, Diet Dr. Pepper and a bag of mini pretzels ought to do the trick.

I had to make an emergency run to Food Lion because I don't keep such stuff in my house. I don't keep such stuff in my house because I know it's not good for me. Needless to say, I make a lot of emergency runs to Food Lion.

As I pulled out of the parking lot, I saw Beer-man. He didn't seem to be headed toward any car, so apparently he had walked to the store. It's a good thing, I thought.

He approached an old man with a cane and I assumed Beer-man was asking the poor, defenseless man for money. Oh, leave the old guy alone!

Then after a brief conversation, Beer-man smiled broadly, took the empty shopping cart from the old man and returned it to the cart rack for him.

That's when my judgmentalism smacked me in the face.

In the course of a typical day, I wonder how many judgmental assumptions I make about other people. I've come to the conclusion that it brings me great comfort to identify their problems without even knowing them as people. No doubt they do have problems, because we all do, but I can't begin to know what they are. Still, it makes me feel better about myself when I can feel superior to other people, so this is what I do, usually without thinking about it. But I thought about it that morning.

The truth is, the only person in my little Saturday morning at Food Lion scenario with a problem that I could identify with certainty was me.

Without the meaning I discovered during this quick shopping excursion, I would have long forgotten it. The meaning I attach to my stories is more important for me than the stories themselves. In big and small ways, that meaning changes the way I see the world, myself and my relationship with God.

~

I hope that within these pages you haven't heard me say that everything happens for a reason, or that God is somehow manipulating the minute details of our lives to teach us lessons. I can't begin to understand why some things happen. I can't bring myself to say that God makes everything happen for a reason. I *can* say that everything we experience has potential meaning. Within the threads of our stories, we have opportunities to pull meaning from the tangled mess.

Like pulling threads from the tangled mess, meaning-making is not neat and tidy. Some threads are in plain sight, some are partially revealed, and others are well hidden. Sometimes two threads are harmoniously entwined, or they may be so tightly tangled that they contradict one another. Some threads glide away from the mess like an irrefutable truth, some stubbornly remain hidden, and others tease us by freeing themselves as we tug on one end until it becomes apparent that the other end will remain forever melded into the mess. Some threads of meaning are retrievable and some aren't.

When we ask, "What does this mean?" and the question goes unanswered, it can be maddening. I suspect that all of us who search for deeper meaning in our lives confront meaninglessness.

But here's the thing. And it's a really big thing. When our stories seem meaningless, they may hold the deepest meaning of all for us.

When meaning eludes us, we're ready to grapple with ambiguity, paradox and mystery. We can neither pretend nor presume to understand them, just as we can neither pretend nor presume to understand God.

Don't dismiss the absence of meaning as worthless. Allow it to become a part of the deeper meaning of your story. This is as close as you'll ever come to grasping the One who is ungraspable.

The mystery that is God can never be understood. Once you presume to understand God, God ceases to be a mystery and God ceases to be God. Relish the mystery that's present in the absence of meaning.

~

Pulling meaning from the tangled mess isn't easy work. It involves struggle, uncertainty, honesty and pain, but it's worth the effort.

Along the way, we discover that the time we spend on this earth is more than a series of events marking our lives like headstones in a cemetery. Beneath our stories lies a depth of meaning waiting to be uncovered. Beyond that meaning lies an even deeper truth that connects us to the divine Story we share with one another and all creation.

In the midst of struggle, doubt, joy, heartbreak, embarrassment, disillusionment, wonderment, wisdom, tragedy, humor and surprise, may you pull threads of meaning from the tangled mess, and may those threads connect you to the larger Thread that runs through all our lives.

Acknowledgements

⟨⟨◦⟩⟩

This book is the result of a long process that began with a number of dear friends who encouraged me to write it. I thank them for their nudges along the way. In particular, it was the prodding of Peg Robarchek and her generous offer to assist me that got me going. I can't thank her enough for sharing her wisdom and insight into the process of writing. She actually persuaded me that I am an author, which was no easy task. As a Sunday morning preacher and a blogger, I knew I was a writer, but an author is a different animal, and I had to be convinced that I was up to the task.

I am grateful to my proofreaders for their suggestions and first class nitpicking: Sheila Chapman Liles, Lucille (CeCee) Mills, Elaine Rhodes, Karen Dawson Haag and Lennie Richardson. And special appreciation goes to Mitch Roof, who had to deal with my uncooperative mug for photos.

I thank the people of Trinity Lutheran Church in Jamestown, North Dakota; Emmanuel in Kilgore, Ohio; Trinity in Carrollton, Ohio; Advent in Uniontown, Ohio; and Advent in Charlotte, North Carolina, for walking with me for a time and teaching me the meaning of grace. Most of all, my deepest appreciation goes to the dear saints and sinners of Holy Trinity Lutheran Church in Charlotte for inspiring me to be a better person and loving me even when I'm not.

Nancy Kraft
June 2015